When Performance Stalls

Six Levers for Fixing the Work

So Teams Can Perform

Jennifer Lilly

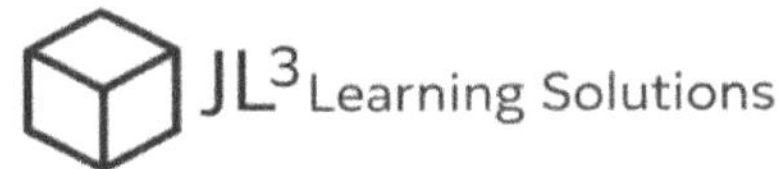

When Performance Stalls: Six Levers for Fixing the Work So Teams Can Perform

Artificial intelligence tools were used during the drafting and editing process to assist with language refinement, structural suggestions, and idea exploration. Final decisions regarding content, structure, and language were made solely by the author.

Illustrations in this book were generated using artificial intelligence based on original concepts, prompts, and creative direction provided by the author. Final image selection and use were determined by the author.

ISBN 979-8-9955457-0-5 (Paperback)
ISBN 979-8-9955457-1-2 (Hardcover)

First Edition

Cover design by Jennifer Lilly

Published by JL³ Learning Solutions
Knoxville, Iowa

For inquiries, visit www.jl3learningsolutions.com

Contents

Introduction

Most leaders have experienced it.

A team is capable. The people are engaged. They care about the work and want to do it well. And yet, results are inconsistent. Deadlines slip. Errors repeat. Performance depends too heavily on who is doing the work.

When this happens, the response is predictable. Leaders focus on the people. They call for more accountability, more communication, more training. Sometimes those efforts help. Often, they do not. The same problems return, just in different forms.

This book starts from a different premise.

When capable, committed people are not producing consistent results, the issue is rarely motivation. More often, the issue is the design of the work itself.

Work is not neutral. It creates conditions. Those conditions shape what people do, how consistently they do it, and how much effort it takes to perform well. When those conditions are misaligned, even strong teams struggle. When they are designed well, performance becomes more predictable and less dependent on individual effort alone.

This book will show you how to identify and change those conditions.

The JL^3 Performance Levers™ provide a practical way to diagnose what is shaping performance in your environment and to make targeted changes that improve results. Instead of asking, "Why aren't people performing?" you will learn to ask, "What about the work is making performance harder or easier?"

The story in Part I follows a leadership team working through these questions in real time. It is designed to help you see how performance problems develop and how they are often misunderstood.

Part II introduces the six levers directly. Each lever represents a condition that influences performance. As you move through them, you will be able to examine your own work environment and identify where misalignment is affecting results.

You can read this book straight through, or you can return to specific sections as you work through a real performance challenge. The goal is not just understanding. The goal is to give you a way to see your work differently and make decisions that lead to more consistent performance.

Because when the work is designed well, people do not just work harder.

They perform.

Chapter 1: Return to River & Ridge

"The more you look, the more you see."

– Robert M. Pirsig, *Zen and the Art of Motorcycle Maintenance*

The bell over the door at River & Ridge Outfitters gave a single, tired jingle. Then the shop settled around Jenna: pine wax, hot coffee, and the damp nylon smell of rain shells hanging by the door. Screens along the back wall looped hikers on bright ridgelines, but the videos felt more upbeat than the store itself did that Saturday morning. Above the entrance, a poster declared ADVENTURE STARTS HERE, sun-faded to near gray. Someone had pinned a "20% OFF SOCKS" coupon over the S in STARTS.

For a moment, the poster pulled her backward. She could still remember standing near this same doorway as a girl, watching her mother greet customers before they ever reached the counter and her father straighten displays no one else would have noticed were off by half an inch. Back then, the store had felt busy in a way that held together. Now her parents were retired, and River & Ridge belonged to her in every way that mattered. That was exactly why she was here.

Jenna stepped inside and moved like any other customer. That was the point of today. No clipboard. No introduction. She did not want anyone changing how they worked because she was there. She drifted toward a rack of rain jackets and ran her fingers along a seam. Then she lifted a tag and studied it for a moment. Her pace stayed slow and casual. She wanted to look interested, but not committed, like someone still deciding whether anything in the store was worth buying.

The counter sat to her left, a rectangle of scuffs and coffee rings. A young clerk stood at the register: soft jawline, name tag turned halfway around, hair flattened by a backward cap. He lifted his eyes and offered a practiced smile that did not quite reach them.

"Hey," he said. "Holler if you need anything."

"Thanks," Jenna said. She took another step toward the packs and paused as if she had just remembered something. "I'm looking for a day pack that won't hurt my shoulders. Maybe something in the twenty-five to thirty liter range, women's fit if you've got it, and comfortable enough for a long day hike?"

He tipped his chin toward the wall of packs. "They're over there."

Jenna followed his nod and waited, just long enough to see whether he would come with her. He did not. His gaze dropped back to the register screen, thumb flicking at the keys with practiced indifference. She smiled, turned back, and lifted the strap of a women's-frame pack to feel the padding. "Any favorites?" she asked.

He sighed, not irritated exactly, just done with the question before it finished landing. "I mean... I just work here."

The words were not hostile. They were familiar. Jenna nodded without reacting. "Don't we all," she said quietly.

She slipped the cardboard sleeve off her coffee cup and, using the pen she kept tucked behind her ear, made a small dot in the margin. Next to it, she wrote, "I just work here." Then she added, ownership gap. Below that, she drew two circles and labeled them Role and Identity. She left a narrow space between them.

Near the maps, a display of bear canisters stood like blue helmets guarding the guidebooks. A middle-aged couple hovered nearby with glossy trail maps in their hands.

"We're thinking Indian Peaks," the woman said to a staffer at the endcap. "Do we need a permit?"

"Two weeks in advance," the staffer said, tapping a laminated photo of Alpine Lakes. "Minimum. They go fast."

The couple's faces fell. "We fly back Monday," the man said.

A voice came from farther down the aisle, a local by the sound of him and by the wear on his jacket. He cleared his throat. "Sorry," he said gently, "day use opens at five p.m. the day before. You've still got a shot if you get on it right away." He raised a hand in apology. "Overnight permits are the ones you have to plan further out."

The staffer blinked. "Oh. Right. I... thought they changed it the other way."

"They changed it last spring," the man said. He sounded almost embarrassed to know. "Granddaughter and I go most weeks."

Relief loosened the couple's shoulders. "Thank you," the woman said. "We'll set an alarm."

"Good luck," the local said. Then he stepped back and pretended to check a price tag so the employee would not feel embarrassed.

Jenna took in the exchange. The mistake was small, but it still mattered. On the sleeve she wrote: Permit policy wrong. Training drift. Credibility hit. Then, after a brief pause, she added: Bright spot: local knowledge in the store.

Beyond the maps, the pack-fitting corner held a mirror and a small riser platform. A tall employee with an easy grin knelt to tighten the hip belt on a teenage boy whose hair had settled into a shape that looked both proud and unruly.

"Okay," the employee said, her voice light and steady, "we want the weight on your pelvis, not your shoulders. Do you feel the shift?"

The boy's expression changed immediately. Doubt gave way to interest, then relief. "Oh. Yeah. That's way better."

"Magic of geometry," she said. "Do a lap past the tents and back. If anything rubs, yell 'ow' dramatically and I'll fix it."

The boy laughed and headed off, stomping a little harder than necessary because he liked how strong he felt. Behind the register, two other employees stood shoulder to shoulder over their phones, thumbs moving fast, private smiles on both faces. The fitter looked in their direction for a brief second, the way someone checks for a problem before deciding whether to intervene, then turned back to the pack wall.

Jenna stepped closer. "You're good at this," she said.

The fitter stood and rolled one shoulder. "Guide seasons," she said. "And I like puzzles. Humans are puzzles with feet."

Jenna smiled. "That's a good line."

The fitter gave a small half shrug toward the counter, where the phone glow made the inattention harder to miss. "We do some training, but you know how it goes when things get busy. Most days, the floor trains you."

Jenna wrote a note along the edge of the sleeve: Different employees, different standards. One fitter is careful and skilled. Others are distracted. Unclear what the store actually reinforces. She drew a star beside the note.

Near the rentals window, a couple in matching windbreakers walked up carrying hiking gear. They looked tired in the specific way people do after spending the whole day trying to handle things correctly.

“We just need to pay for an extra rental day,” the man told the rentals associate.

“Oh, returns go to the front,” the associate said, pointing toward the registers. “They handle all payments.”

The couple carried the gear to the front counter. The clerk there, a person with curly hair and a patient expression, gave a small wince. “I need the rentals intake sheet before I can check anything in,” he said. “That part goes through the rentals desk.”

“But he said you could,” the woman began, then stopped herself. A second later she smiled the way people do when something simple turns out not to be simple. “Okay. Back we go.”

“I’m so sorry,” the clerk said. He sounded sincere and slightly embarrassed. “I’ll call the rentals desk.”

He picked up the phone at the front counter and placed the call. Three feet behind him, the phone at the rentals window rang while no one answered it.

The couple turned back toward rentals, then toward the front again, stuck in a slow loop. No one was rude. Everyone was just handling their own piece. Jenna wrote: Payment ping-pong. Process handoff has no owner. She boxed the note, then drew one long arrow and wrote above it: one flow.

A whiteboard hung beside the rentals door. MORNING HUDDLE was written across the top in large block letters that had started to lose their edge. Below it were bullet points: Sat. Staffing. Weekend Promo. Trail Advisory. The advisory read: Mon: icy north faces; microspikes rec. The corner said Mon 10/20. Today was Saturday, and it was not the twentieth.

Jenna brushed a fingerprint off the board with her sleeve and looked at the streak it left. The board was still directing people with information that no longer applied. On the sleeve she wrote: Whiteboard out of date. Old information still shaping decisions.

At checkout, the line moved in patient starts and stops. A man buying socks for every possible temperature chatted about elk in the foothills. A student with a climbing guidebook rehearsed knots with a scrap of cord while he waited. The card reader beeped, blinked, and displayed an error.

"Sorry," the curly-haired clerk said, pressing his lips together in apology. "She's got a personality."

"What's the trick?" the man asked, good-natured.

"Cancel, chip, tap, then we both hold our breath for three seconds." He tapped through the sequence. "Okay. One, two, three. Try again."

They did. It worked. Everyone in line exhaled.

When Jenna stepped up with a pack of blister pads and a trail map she did not need, the clerk offered an embarrassed half smile. “One day it’ll just work,” he said. “Today isn’t that day.”

“Maybe it likes an audience,” Jenna said.

“Then it’s in the right store.” He handed her the bag like a small apology. “We’re slammed at noon. Come back for the fireworks.”

“I’ll bring popcorn,” Jenna said.

She took three slow steps toward the door and let the room register one more time. The fitter adjusting the teenager’s pack with practiced accuracy. The young clerk’s shoulders turning inward toward the register. Signs that told customers to CHECK IN HERE and START THERE within the same line of sight. The whiteboard is still offering Monday’s trail warning to Saturday customers. A back door that stuck and then thudded shut.

“Have we met?” someone said behind her.

The senior guide from the wall photos stood near the end of the counter. His face still looked direct even when he was not smiling. Weather and time had left fine lines beside his eyes.

“You look familiar,” he said, as if familiarity were worth checking.

“Probably just have one of those faces,” Jenna said, keeping her tone light.

He nodded politely, though he clearly did not fully buy the answer. “Well, welcome in,” he said. “If you need trail information or current conditions, ask for one of the guides.”

"Thanks," Jenna said.

Outside, the day had that clear high-altitude brightness that makes the edges of things look sharp. The Flatirons cut a clean silhouette against the sky. Jenna sat on a bench by the planter box where the hemlock did not quite thrive and balanced her coffee on her knee. She finished the last usable inch of the sleeve.

She flipped it over and wrote a clean column, letting each line stand on its own:

> "I just work here."
> Permit info wrong. Customer corrected it.
> Strong fitter; standards split.
> Payment ping-pong.
> Whiteboard out of date.
> Card reader ritual.

Beneath the list, she wrote six short headings for herself: mindset, skill, norms, capacity, cues, tools. A way to sort what she was seeing before she knew how much of it would hold.

Her pen hovered above the sleeve for a moment. The people were trying. That was clear. The work around them was making success harder than it needed to be.

She slid the sleeve into the pocket of the folded map. The bell over the door jingled again as another customer stepped inside. Jenna stood and followed the sidewalk past the bike rack, then around the corner to the alley where deliveries came in. She was not leaving yet. She wanted to see the store from another side.

In the alley's shade, the building looked more straightforward: cinderblock walls, old metal conduit, and a stack of boxes near the edge of a propped-open door, their cardboard darkened by damp air. A sticker on the door read GUIDES ONLY, but the door stood open a hand's width. Voices drifted out from inside, steady most of the time, with brief bursts of complaint.

"...schedule changed again?" a voice said.

"Email at seven-thirty," another voice answered. "I was already in the canyon."

A third voice said, "I told the floor manager last week we needed a printed board with the week at a glance."

"The floor manager told me that was Ops," the first voice replied. "Ops told me to ask the floor manager."

A short laugh followed. Not mean. Not especially patient either. Something metal clanged against something else.

Jenna stayed where she was and listened.

"Did the fitter get that kid fitted?" the third voice asked, and this time there was pride in it.

"Perfect," said the second voice without hesitation. "The kid stood taller when he walked out."

"Of course he did," the first voice said. "She should be teaching fittings, not covering returns."

"We're short on returns," someone said, and the warmth thinned.

A cart rattled. Boots thudded. "Where do you want these?" a new voice asked. The answer overlapped with a phone ringing. The ringing stopped. No one said hello. Then it started again.

Jenna stayed another minute, listening to the work away from the sales floor. Then she circled back to the front. The senior guide was finishing a conversation with a customer and glanced up when he saw her, the look of someone still trying to place a face.

"You're still here," he said.

"Trying to decide whether I like the map more than the idea of the map," Jenna said.

He chuckled. "Can I give you a tip?"

"Please."

"If you want the best loop for a long day that doesn't feel too long, start at Fourth Street instead of the main trailhead. Fewer people. Same ridge."

"I like the sound of a long day that doesn't wear you out too fast," Jenna said. "That's a useful distinction."

The senior guide's eyes warmed. "You guide?" he asked. More observation than question.

"Long time ago," she said. "In other mountains."

He nodded once. "Figures."

Inside, the store had shifted from morning quiet to mid-morning traffic. The two employees behind the counter had traded phones for a stack of returns. The fitter stood at the pack wall refitting the same teenager, who now wore the careful expression of someone trying to remember what good felt like. The card reader failed twice, then cooperated. The whiteboard still offered Monday's conditions to Saturday.

Jenna let herself become one more body in the store for a few minutes, then stepped aside when a family with a stroller needed room at the door. She took a seat at the window bar and opened the trail map flat in front of her, not because she needed it, but because it gave her a reason to stay.

On a clean page of her pocket notebook, she wrote:

First pass:

> Mindset: "I just work here."
> Skill: Staffer gives wrong permit information; customer corrects it.
> Norms: One employee's excellence beside phone-scroll drift.
> Capacity: Rentals to front to rentals loop; nobody owns the handoff.
> Cues: Outdated whiteboard notes.
> Tools: Card reader requires ritual and luck.

Under that, she drew a simple swimlane sketch with four labeled sections: Rentals, Front, Guide Desk, Floor. Then she marked an X where the work crossed from one lane to another and stalled.

In her head, she replaced the idea of fixing everything with two questions she trusted more. Where is the friction highest? What is the smallest change that would bring real relief?

She folded the map neatly and slid it, along with the sleeve, into her tote. When the clock on the wall struck noon, the store shifted again. The senior guide came out from the back and joined the front, moving with the kind of calm efficiency that got more done than visible rushing. The young clerk from earlier straightened, noticed the line, and, Jenna noted, stepped toward the nearest customer without being told. He did not see her watching. She did not write that down. Not yet.

A woman in a polo with the store logo came out from the back carrying a stack of printed schedules. On her way through, she stopped at the whiteboard and uncapped a dry-erase marker. She looked at the date, frowned, and erased Mon 10/20 with a few quick, embarrassed swipes. Then she scanned the room for somewhere to put the marker, settled on the edge of the frame, and turned back to the floor.

“Team,” the floor manager called, not loudly, but with the kind of voice people responded to without argument. “Quick reset at three by the pack wall.”

Heads lifted. Nods. The fitter raised a thumb without looking up from a sternum strap.

Jenna watched the instruction land and the work continue. It was a small moment, but it told her something important. This might be a place where change could take hold.

When the rush eased and the line shortened, Jenna stood and moved toward the door. The bell jingled again, sharper this time under the noon traffic. Outside, the sidewalk carried a steady stream of Boulder residents in sandals and trail runners, dogs on leashes, laptops slung over shoulders. The Flatirons still held the skyline.

She took the side street toward the coffee shop on the corner and settled at a back table where the espresso machine punctuated the room with short bursts of steam. Her notebook sat in the light, ready.

End-of-day journal – R&R

> Walked as a customer. No announcement.
> Collected six signals: mindset, skill, norms, capacity, cues, tools.
> Observed one strong bright spot: skilled fitter at pack wall.
> Heard one phrase that explains disengagement: "I just work here."
> Saw one leadership signal: floor manager called a reset and people responded.
> Senior guide = trusted voice. Possible bridge.

She turned the page. The pen paused above the paper. There was always a moment when she had to decide how directly to name what she was seeing. She could make it softer. She could make it sharper. Both could be true.

She chose the version that felt accurate and fair.

The people are trying. The work is not doing enough to help them succeed.

She wrote one more line beneath it.

That can be redesigned.

She closed the notebook and rested her hand on the cover for a moment. The espresso machine hissed. Out on the street, the day kept moving. In an hour, she would walk back and stop being a customer.

For now, she finished her coffee and folded the map she already knew by heart, a person buying maps not to learn a place, but to study how to help it work better.

Chapter 2: Welcome to Twin Lakes

"Without reflection, we go blindly on our way."

– Margaret J. Wheatley

The next morning, Jenna flipped through the pages of her notebook, coffee-stained and crowded with arrows, quick sketches, and half-formed thoughts. Early light came in cold through the office window. Outside, frost still clung to the branches, catching the sun in thin silver lines.

She read the same notes again.

- "I just work here."
- Wrong permit information corrected by a customer.
- One strong employee carrying a standard that did not clearly exist around her.

- Customers passed between counters because no one owned the handoff.
- Old information still posted where people were expected to rely on it.
- A tool that only worked if someone already knew its quirks.

Each note pointed back to the same broader problem. The people were not careless. They were not checked out. They were trying to do good work inside routines, systems, and expectations that no longer supported the work clearly enough.

She rubbed her temples.

When the work is poorly designed, good people start looking inconsistent.

That line had come to her in the coffee shop the day before, and it had not left her.

The radiator clicked softly in the corner. Jenna opened her laptop and started a new document. It was not a report. It was not yet a plan. It was a place to sort what she was seeing before the details blurred together.

At the top, she typed:

What's really getting in the way?

Then she began listing what she already knew.

People care, but they do not all seem connected to the purpose of the work in the same way.

Skill exists, but it is uneven, and too much of it depends on who happened to teach whom.

The team adapts constantly, but not always in the same direction.

Work gets handed off without clear ownership.

The environment sends mixed signals about what matters most.

Tools and processes require memory, workarounds, and extra interpretation.

She leaned back and read the list.

Not chaos. Pattern.

Six recurring areas. Six places where the work either supported people or made success harder than it needed to be.

She circled each one and wrote the clearest labels she had for them so far.

- Mindset Alignment – how people understand priorities
- Skill Readiness – what they are prepared to do
- Peer Norms – what the group reinforces in practice
- Shared Capacity – how work and strain are distributed
- System Cues – what the environment signals and rewards
- Tool Support – what the process and tools hold, or fail to hold

The labels helped, but she did not mistake them for the work itself. Naming something too early could make it sound simpler than it was. If this was going to matter, the team would need to recognize it in their own experience, not just hear her describe it.

Jenna closed the document and opened a new message.

> Subject: Leadership Offsite – Twin Lakes Lodge
>
> We've been pushing hard for a long time. It's time to pause, reflect, and rethink how we lead together.
>
> Join me this week at Twin Lakes Lodge. Pack light, bring layers, and leave your laptop behind.
>
> We are not going to push harder. We are going to find a better way forward.
>
> Jenna

She read it once, then clicked Send.

The message went to six people, the ones with enough influence to change how River & Ridge actually worked if they were willing to look honestly at it.

Caleb, Director of Operations, was halfway through his second spreadsheet of the morning when the email landed. The tap of his pen stopped mid-rhythm. He believed every problem had a structure if you looked hard enough, but lately even his cleanest systems had started breaking down under the weight of exceptions. Another retreat. He exhaled through his nose. If there was no plan attached, he would probably end up making one himself.

Lena, HR and Culture Lead, read the subject line and leaned back in her chair. Her coffee sat beside her, already cool. She had helped lead more resets than she cared to count, most of them sincere, some of them useful, few of them lasting. But she trusted Jenna's instincts. And some tired part of her still wanted this one to be different.

Marcus, Sales and Partnerships Lead, was in the middle of a call when the notification flashed across his phone. A week-long retreat. He smirked and leaned back in his chair while city noise drifted faintly through the window. Nothing like an offsite to interrupt a quarter. Still, Jenna's tone caught his attention. It sounded less corporate than usual. Less polished. He muted the call long enough to read it again.

Theo, Customer Experience Manager, laughed when he saw it. "Guess the boss wants to play camp counselor," he joked to a frontline rep passing by. The break room smelled like fryer oil and coffee. But the final line — find a better way forward — stayed with him. He had spent years watching employees work around systems that made good service harder than it needed to be. If Jenna was serious, maybe this was worth the drive.

Sofia, Finance and Strategy Analyst, blinked at the message and read it twice. She was not usually on lists like this. The printer near her desk hummed steadily in the background. As the youngest person in most rooms like this, she still sometimes felt as though she had to earn the right to be there before speaking. But the invitation was clear. She replied, I'm in, before she could overthink it.

Priya, Training and Development Lead, read it at the edge of a cluttered desk with two binders open and sticky notes layered over one another like a second document. She smiled as she reread the line about leaving laptops behind. It sounded like Jenna. Practical, but not performative. Priya had been noticing inconsistencies for months. The same job was being taught differently, understood differently, and producing different outcomes. She had not yet found the right way to pull the pattern together. Maybe this would help.

Back in her office, Jenna refreshed her inbox.

The replies came one by one.

> I'll be there.
> I'm in.
> Do we need hiking boots?
> Please tell me there's coffee.

She smiled. Six yeses.

On the yellow pad beside her keyboard, she underlined the six labels she had written earlier, then drew a loose circle around them. Not a finished model. More like a working map.

Before closing her laptop, she scheduled one more message to herself for after the retreat. Something brief enough that she would still read it when she was tired.

> Subject: After the summit

> Remember: We are not fixing people. We are changing the conditions around the work.

She closed the screen, slipped the notebook into her bag, and reached for her jacket.

By the time Jenna left Boulder, the sun had already started its slow drop west. She drove for hours, trading traffic and storefronts for highway, then two-lane mountain road, then the last stretch of gravel that led toward Twin Lakes. The farther she climbed, the quieter it got. Ponderosa pine replaced neighborhoods. She reached over and turned the radio off, leaving only the sound of the road.

By late afternoon, the mountains had shifted from silver to slate. The road narrowed as her SUV climbed higher. Snowmelt had left thin ribbons of ice in the shadows. When the trees finally opened, the lodge appeared ahead of her, timbered and weathered, tucked against the slope with its roofline angled toward the peaks beyond. Smoke trailed from the stone chimney and dissolved into the cold air.

The lake stretched below it, still enough to reflect the last of the light. In the distance, Mount Elbert held the horizon, its ridgeline catching the fading pink of sunset.

Jenna parked near the edge of the drive and stepped out. The cold cut quickly through her gloves. She welcomed it. It had a way of stripping away mental clutter.

Inside, the lodge felt older than the store, and steadier. Rough-hewn beams crossed the ceiling. A stone fireplace anchored the room.

Leather chairs, worn rugs, framed maps, and black-and-white photographs made the place feel less like a venue and more like a place people returned to on purpose.

Caleb arrived first, exactly on time, carrying a laptop bag despite the instruction not to. His boots looked almost unused.

Lena came next, scarf wrapped twice around her neck, taking in the room with the relieved look of someone who had needed quiet more than she had realized.

Marcus walked in still finishing a call over Bluetooth, then frowned at his phone when the signal dropped and slid it into his pocket with visible reluctance.

Priya arrived with a folder under one arm and apologized for being "slightly overprepared," which made Theo laugh the moment he stepped through the door behind her.

Theo's truck announced itself before he did, engine louder than necessary, his grin following him inside.

Sofia came last. She paused just inside the doorway for half a second, taking everything in before stepping fully into the room.

They set their bags near the entry and gathered around the fire, carrying the usual awkwardness that comes with stepping out of daily roles without yet knowing what replaces them. No one seemed sure whether to talk about work or pretend work was not already in the room.

Jenna poured coffee into mismatched mugs and passed them out.

"Welcome to Twin Lakes," she said. "We're here to think, to listen, and to find a better way forward."

The fire popped softly. Caleb looked into his mug. Lena waited, pen still in her hand.

Outside, wind moved through the pines and brushed the lodge siding. The mountains stood beyond the windows, not dramatic, just present.

Jenna looked around the room. Guarded faces. Tired faces. Curious faces. People who had been carrying different parts of the same problem for a long time.

Tomorrow, they would start naming what they had all been living inside.

It was not empty. It was the pause before the real work began.

By dusk, the lodge glowed with firelight and the smell of cedar. Someone had cracked a window just enough to let a line of cold air slip in. Dinner was simple: soup in a cast-iron pot, bread warming in the oven, mugs and bowls gathered around the long pine table.

At first, the conversation stayed easy. The drive. The weather. The altitude. Theo made a joke about being officially off the grid the moment his GPS failed. Even Marcus laughed.

When the noise settled, Jenna rested her elbows lightly on the table.

"That was part of the point," she said. "No Wi-Fi. No dashboards. No interruptions. Just us and the conditions shaping the work."

The group exchanged glances.

Caleb shifted in his seat. "So what exactly is this? Strategy? A reset? Team building?"

"Maybe some of all three," Jenna said. "But mostly this is time to look carefully at how we've been working and where that approach has stopped helping us."

She let that settle before continuing.

"We've been pushing hard for a long time. Effort is not the issue. What I'm less convinced about is whether the work around people is supporting the results we say we want."

Lena leaned forward first. "So this isn't about changing personalities."

"No," Jenna said. "It's about looking at the conditions people are working inside."

Priya nodded slowly. Theo sat back but kept his eyes on Jenna. Sofia had already stopped eating and was listening with full attention.

Marcus rotated his mug once between his hands. "And you think the problem is in the system."

Jenna met his eyes. "I think enough of the friction is coming from there that it's worth a closer look."

Theo broke the pause with a half grin. "So no trust falls, then?"

That got a real laugh.

"No trust falls," Jenna said. "Just honest work."

Later, one by one, they rose from the table and drifted toward the fire. Outside, stars had started to appear over the lake. Inside, the room had loosened a little. The hierarchy was still there, but quieter now.

Jenna stood for a moment at the window with her coffee and looked out at the dark outline of the peaks.

Tomorrow, they would begin.

Not by fixing people.

By learning how to see the work more clearly.

Chapter 3: What Matters Most

"If you want to go fast, go alone. If you want to go far, go together."

–African Proverb

The morning light stretched across the lodge's timber floors, thin and golden, catching the steam rising from half-drunk mugs of coffee. The mood was different than the night before, quieter and steadier. Outside, a veil of mist hovered over Twin Lakes, softening the ridgelines in the distance. Somewhere in the trees, a jay called once, then fell silent.

Jenna stood near the stone hearth, her hands wrapped around her mug. The fire was not lit yet. The coals from the night before sat pale and still. She liked it that way, quiet and expectant, like the pause before a long conversation begins.

"We did not come here just to talk," she said. "We came here to understand what is making the work harder than it should be."

Heads lifted. Caleb leaned forward slightly, elbows on the table. Lena was already poised with her notebook, pen hovering above the page.

"When my parents started River & Ridge," Jenna began, "they did not talk about gear or bookings or competition. They talked about moments. My dad used to say the best part of a trip was not the view at the top. It was the look on someone's face when they realized they could do something they never thought they could."

Her voice softened with memory. "They started with one raft and a borrowed truck. My mom ran the office from our kitchen table. Their mission was simple: help people grow through challenge. Give them courage they could carry home with them. That was the real business. Confidence passed from one person to another."

A few small smiles moved around the room.

"But somewhere along the way," Jenna continued, "we got busy. We grew, and growth brought more trips, more gear, more logistics. Those were all good things. But when the work gets busy, people start making fast decisions. If they are not clear on what matters most, they make good decisions in different directions."

She set her mug down and turned to the whiteboard. In bold strokes, she wrote:

WHAT MATTERS MOST?

"Before we change any system," she said, "we have to start here. If priorities are unclear, people will solve problems based on their own judgment, their own pressure, and their own assumptions about what should come first."

She wrote a second line beneath it:

When priorities compete, people need to know what comes first.

"Even good teams get misaligned this way," she said. "They still care. The problem is that they are being asked to make tradeoffs without enough guidance. Sometimes we get so busy doing the work that we stop checking whether people are still making decisions from the same understanding of what matters most."

A low chuckle moved through the room. Someone murmured, "That feels familiar."

Jenna nodded. "So today, we're checking direction."

She passed small cards around the table. "Take a few minutes. Don't overthink it. Just write what comes to mind."

On the board, she wrote five questions in thick, deliberate lines:

- What outcome matters most when the work gets busy?
- When speed, quality, and guest experience compete, which one should win first?
- Where are people being forced to make tradeoffs without enough guidance?
- What work needs more time, attention, or support if we are serious about that priority?
- What are leaders saying matters most, and where do our choices fail to match it?

"These are not mission questions," Jenna said. "They are priority questions."

The room grew quiet. Pens began moving across the cards. Outside, a light breeze stirred the birch trees near the porch, and the leaves brushed softly against one another. Inside, the only other sound was the steady scratch of handwriting.

After a minute, Lena looked up. "So... are you saying we've been headed in the wrong direction?"

Jenna tilted her head. "Not exactly. I'm saying we may not have been clear enough about what should guide decisions when the work gets crowded. And when people stop checking that, their work starts pulling toward different definitions of success."

Across the table, Theo leaned forward. “Feels like we’re still trying to get people outside and give them a good time. That’s still the goal, right?”

“It is,” Jenna said. “But having a good time is not the purpose. It’s the result. The purpose is what makes the experience matter. The question now is whether our people know what to protect first when that experience starts competing with efficiency, speed, volume, or cost. If we stop naming that clearly, then each team starts filling in the answer on its own.”

The group fell quiet again.

Caleb looked toward the window. The morning light softened against the glass, and for a moment Twin Lakes faded from his attention. Another scene rose in its place, older and sharper.

He remembered the smell of pine and wet snow. Mount Elbert, early spring. The first clear Saturday after the thaw.

He and several other senior guides had gone up that morning for a preseason conditioning hike. There were no guests, no tight schedule, no real pressure. The plan was simple: get in a fast climb and shake off the winter slowdown. They had done it so many times that no one treated the day like it required much attention. No full briefing. No map review. No discussion of who was carrying what.

They all knew the mountain.

The first few miles were easy. Laughter. Teasing. Boots moving over thawing ground. Ice cracking in shallow pools beside the trail. But somewhere above timberline, the familiar cairn was gone. Spring runoff had cut a new gully through the slope and split the route in two.

"Left looks right," someone joked, and the group laughed.

Caleb motioned forward. They would sort it out as they went.

The sun climbed higher and burned through the last of the fog. They kept moving, each person choosing the line that looked most natural. As the slope widened, the group spread out without meaning to. One guide drifted toward the saddle. Another angled higher across loose rock.

From below, Caleb could still see everyone. Small figures against the mountain. Each one confident. Each one moving in a slightly different direction.

Then the fog came back.

It rolled in quickly, thick enough to blur distance and flatten sound. Voices faded. For a while, all he could hear was the scrape of boots against stone and his own breathing.

When the fog finally lifted, they were scattered. Three small silhouettes moved toward the ridge from three separate approaches. Caleb reached the summit first, but when the others arrived, no one celebrated. They had all made it. Still, the top felt wrong.

He remembered standing there in the wind, looking out across the ridgeline. Everyone was present, but the usual feeling at the end of a climb was gone. The shared energy that normally came with reaching the top had been replaced by something thinner. They had arrived, but they had not arrived together.

That night, sitting beside his truck, Caleb unfolded the topographic map that had stayed untouched in his pack all day. The contour lines crossed the page in clean, exact patterns. He had not used them. None of them had.

Earlier, they had felt unnecessary.

Now they looked like something important they had ignored.

We were not off because the mountain changed, he realized. We were off because we had not agreed on what mattered most once conditions changed.

When the memory loosened, the lodge came back into focus. He heard the scrape of a chair, the soft hiss of the heater kicking on, the smell of coffee cooling on the table. His pen was still in his hand, unmoving.

He looked up. "Jenna," he said quietly, "I think I know what you mean."

The others turned toward him.

He leaned forward, elbows on his knees, voice steady. "A few years ago, we did a conditioning climb on Mount Elbert. We knew it too well, or thought we did. We skipped the briefing. We didn't review the route. Nobody checked who was carrying what. We just started moving."

He told them about the washed-out trail, the fog, and the way the group had gradually spread apart as each person followed the line that seemed right.

"We all made it to the top," he said, "but it didn't feel like success. Nobody celebrated. We got there, but not in the same way and not for the same reason."

Caleb's pen stopped moving.

Caleb took a breath. "That's what this has started to feel like. We know the work. We know the routines. But when conditions change, I don't think we've been clear enough about what should matter most in the moment."

Jenna nodded, her expression calm. "That is exactly what misalignment looks like when it starts."

She turned back to the board and wrote beneath WHAT MATTERS MOST?

Alignment = Shared Priorities

"Purpose tells you why the work matters," she said. "Alignment tells you what should guide decisions when tradeoffs appear."

The room stayed still for a moment before Priya spoke. She spent more time than anyone translating strategy into training, process, and day-to-day execution.

"It's strange," she said. "You can feel drift even when the numbers still look good. We hit our turnaround goals last quarter, but half my team is just checking boxes. They do the work. They don't always know what it adds up to."

Lena nodded. "Same in guest services. We track satisfaction scores, but it's become transactional. 'Did you enjoy your trip?' is not the same as 'Did this experience change something for you?' We've lost language for the second question."

"Maybe we over-systemized it," Theo said. "We standardized every route and every safety script. That was useful, up to a point. But eventually it started feeling flat. The heart of it got buried under consistency."

A few quiet sounds of agreement circled the room.

Jenna folded her arms. "So what's the response?"

Caleb answered first. "Operations wants efficiency. Marketing wants volume. Guides want experience. None of that is wrong."

"Right," Jenna said. "But if those priorities compete, which one wins first?"

Marcus shifted in his chair, but he did not answer.

Marcus shifted in his seat. "I mean... that probably depends."

"Sometimes," Jenna said. "But not as often as we pretend. If people keep facing the same tradeoff and making different choices, that usually means we have not made the priority clear enough."

Sofia looked toward the board. "And maybe we haven't supported it clearly enough either."

Jenna turned. "Say more."

Sofia sat up a little straighter. "If we say guest experience matters most, then our staffing, scheduling, training time, and equipment decisions should show it. But if we keep spreading time and money across everything like it all matters equally, people are going to assume speed or volume matters just as much."

A murmur of agreement moved around the table.

Priya nodded. "That's true. We say we care about consistency, but then we rush onboarding, trim practice time, and expect people to learn in the gaps."

Theo added, "And we say guest experience matters, but when the day gets packed, what people feel pressure to protect first is the schedule."

Caleb rubbed his jaw. "Which means people are making judgment calls without enough clarity about what should matter most."

"Exactly," Jenna said. "Mindset alignment is not just shared belief. It is shared understanding about what takes priority and where support needs to go when everything cannot win at once."

Lena tapped her pen once against her notebook. "So alignment is not about everyone working the same way. It's about making sure different roles know what should matter most when they have to choose."

Jenna nodded. "Exactly. People can do different work in different ways, but they still need a shared understanding of what they are protecting first. That is what keeps different roles making decisions from the same logic, even when the pressure looks different from one department to the next."

Theo frowned thoughtfully. "Then we need to do a better job of helping people see that connection. Half my department thinks they're just moving inventory. They don't always see how what they do shapes the guest experience."

"What would help?" Jenna asked.

Theo thought for a moment. "Clarity earlier. Clearer priority guidance. And more honesty about tradeoffs. If the expectation is that guest confidence comes before speed, then people need permission to act like that is true."

"That's good," Priya said. "And maybe short weekly resets. Not just purpose reminders. Priority reminders. What matters most this week? Where are people likely to feel a pull in another direction? What support do they need?"

Jenna wrote their phrases on the board:

Clear priorities
Tradeoff guidance
Resource support
Weekly resets

Caleb looked at the words. “That makes sense,” he said. “People do not need the same job. They need the same understanding of what comes first.”

The sentence settled in the room.

Jenna set the marker down. “So maybe the question is not whether we care about the mission,” she said. “Maybe the question is whether we have made our priorities clear enough, and supported them well enough, for people to make consistent decisions.”

Priya let out a slow breath. “We’ve been producing results,” she said. “But it hasn’t felt connected for a while.”

“And that matters,” Jenna said. “Because people can work hard for a long time without clear priorities. They just cannot make consistently strong decisions together if they are each using a different definition of what matters most.”

She gestured toward the wall, where she had already written Guest Experience across the top. Beside her sat a stack of index cards and a cup of sharpened pencils.

“Let’s make this concrete,” she said. “Take a card and write three things. First, the most important outcome your role should protect. Second, the tradeoff you face most often. Third, what support, time, or resource would help you protect the right priority more consistently. When you’re done, we’ll go around the table and share them. Then we’ll put them on the wall and draw the connections.”

They bent over their cards, pencils moving. One by one, they wrote down the work they carried, the tension they felt most often, and the support they wished they had when competing priorities showed up.

After that, Jenna invited them to bring the cards to the wall.

She placed them beneath Guest Experience and began drawing lines upward as each person explained the connection. As more cards went up and more lines were added, the picture widened.

Theo's card connected equipment prep to guest confidence, but also named the pressure to move faster than the situation allowed. Priya's connected training consistency to fewer weak handoffs and named protected practice time as the missing support. Caleb's linked operational reliability to trust, but acknowledged how often efficiency pressures distorted field decisions. Lena's showed conflict handled early before it reached the guest, and named time for coaching as a resource that kept the priority from collapsing under urgency. Marcus's card, after a long pause, connected partnerships and growth to keeping the experience accessible and sustainable, but admitted that volume targets sometimes pulled his choices away from quality. Sofia's connected financial clarity to protecting the conditions that made the mission possible at all, and named the need for clearer spending priorities when tradeoffs had to be made.

Each card showed a different responsibility. Together, they revealed not just how the roles connected, but where the tradeoffs were getting murky and where the support was too thin.

Jenna stepped back. “There it is.”

Caleb looked at the wall and smiled faintly. “That’s clearer than I expected.”

Around the room, people studied the lines and arrows. The mood had changed. More open. More grounded.

Jenna moved back toward the hearth. She had not expected the moment to feel emotional, but it did. Watching them trace their work back to the same priority changed the feel of the room.

They were not fixed yet. But they were looking at the work through the same lens again.

“Here’s the thing about mindset alignment,” she said. “It is not something you establish once and then assume will hold. You have to return to it whenever pressure increases, priorities collide, or the work starts pulling people in different directions.”

Lena raised her hand slightly. “So how often do we do this? This kind of check?”

Jenna smiled. “Usually right when it feels least convenient.”

That drew a small ripple of laughter.

Then she added, “Checking priorities does not slow good work down. It helps people protect the right outcome with the time, support, and attention the work actually requires.”

Outside, the fog had lifted. The peaks stood sharp against a pale blue sky. Jenna picked up the unlit fire poker from beside the hearth and tapped it lightly once against the stone.

"Tomorrow," she said, "we'll move from purpose to practice."

Caleb glanced down at his card, then back at the wall. For the first time in months, he felt something steadier than motivation. Not urgency. Not relief. Just clarity.

He slid the card into his notebook and underlined the phrase he had written in small, careful letters at the bottom:

Protect what matters most, especially when the pressure rises.

Then he closed the notebook with a soft snap and looked once more at the wall, where six different roles were finally pointed toward the same understanding of what had to come first.

What This Means in Practice

- If people are making different tradeoffs in the same situation, priorities are not aligned.
- If leaders say several things matter but never make clear what comes first, staff will fill in the gaps themselves.
- If stated priorities do not shape time, staffing, attention, or support, people will follow the practical demands of the work instead.

Apply This to Your Team

- What outcome should win when priorities collide?
- Where are people currently forced to guess what matters most?
- What decisions, resources, or expectations would need to change to make that priority real?

Chapter 4: Prepared...Or Not

"Do the best you can until you know better.

Then when you know better, do better."

– Maya Angelou

The air was colder by the water.

Jenna led them down the narrow path behind the lodge, boots crunching over frost-stiffened needles. The sun was still low, throwing long shadows from the pines. Twin Lakes lay ahead of them, quiet and pale, the surface broken only by a thin line of ripples where a breeze moved across it.

No one spoke much. Mugs of coffee steamed in gloved hands. It was the kind of morning, Jenna thought, that made you notice your own breathing.

She stopped at the edge of the dock and turned to face them. Caleb stood with his hands in his pockets, shoulders square but tired. Lena wrapped her fingers tighter around her mug, watching the light on the water. Marcus bounced his heel against a loose board, as if part of him was still in motion. Priya pulled her jacket closer, eyes alert. Theo squinted toward the far shore. Sofia lingered a half-step back, taking everything in.

"Yesterday," Jenna said, "we talked about purpose and why River & Ridge exists at all."

She was met with a few nods and quiet sounds of agreement.

"Today we're shifting from why we climb to how we climb. Not the mission statement. Not the big-picture language. The actual work. The part that lives in instruction, repetition, and practice."

She let that sit for a moment, then asked, "Before we head back inside, I want you to think about one thing."

She tipped her chin toward them. "What is one task in your department that feels so basic to you that you assume everyone should know how to do it?"

Theo huffed a quiet laugh. Marcus's jaw flexed. Caleb's brow pulled in, already making a mental list.

"I'm not asking you to answer out loud yet," Jenna added. "Just notice what comes to mind. The task that frustrates you when it is done badly. The one you are sure is obvious, even if you have never stopped to define what good performance actually looks like at each stage of learning."

Beside her, small waves lapped against the dock. The sound was quiet and steady.

"The problem with skill," Jenna said, "is that leaders often judge performance without identifying the level. We expect consistency from people who are still learning. We expect judgment from people who still need steps. Then we call it a people problem when the work breaks down."

The wind picked up, tugging at scarves and jackets. Near the far bank, two ducks moved slowly through a patch of reeds, their movement barely disturbing the surface of the lake.

"Hold on to that task," Jenna said. "We're going to use it in a minute. Let's head back up."

They turned toward the lodge as a group, boots thudding against the dock, breath puffing in the cold. Behind them, the lake moved in small, steady waves.

The lodge was warmer than the morning air, but the quiet came in with them. Jenna led the group toward the big pine table and turned to the whiteboard.

She drew a vertical line and made five short marks across it like steps.

"At the simplest level," she said, "skill readiness is this: knowing what level someone is actually operating at and what they need to move to the next level."

Beside the steps, she wrote:

- Novice
- Beginner
- Competent
- Proficient
- Expert

The group read the words in silence.

"This is the ladder we're working with today," Jenna said. "Every task we expect from our teams sits somewhere on this ladder. Every person performing that task also sits somewhere on this ladder. Most leadership frustration starts when we assume someone is higher on the ladder than they really are."

Caleb leaned forward slightly. Sofia was already writing. Marcus crossed his arms.

Jenna tapped the bottom rung. "A novice is brand new. They need exposure, clear explanation, and close guidance."

She tapped the next rung. "A beginner can follow instructions, but still needs reminders, practice, and correction."

Then the center rung. "A competent person can perform the task reliably under normal conditions. They may still need support when something unusual happens, but they can do the work."

She moved higher. "A proficient person can adjust. They recognize patterns. They can handle variation without getting lost."

At the top, she paused. "An expert performs with strong judgment and very little effort. But experts often skip steps when they teach because the work feels obvious to them."

Caleb gave a quiet grunt of recognition.

Jenna nodded. "Exactly."

She turned back to the group. "Now I want us to define these rungs in real terms. Not abstract terms. Pick the task you were thinking about outside. Then ask two questions. What does novice look like for this task? What does expert look like?"

People shifted in their seats and looked back at their notes.

Theo spoke first. "For front desk check-in, novice means they need the script in front of them. They're following steps exactly."

Jenna nodded and wrote it down.

"Beginner," Lena added, "would mean they can do the basic sequence, but they still miss details."

"Competent means they can get a guest checked in correctly without needing help," Priya said. "As long as nothing unusual comes up."

Theo pointed toward her. "Yes. That's right."

"Proficient," Sofia said quietly, "would mean they can handle exceptions. Missing forms. Wrong reservation details. A late arrival."

"And expert," Caleb added, "means they can do all that and also teach someone else without skipping steps."

Jenna underlined the last phrase. "Without skipping steps. That matters."

She looked around the room. "We're not just naming the task. We're defining the levels of performance inside the task."

Marcus shifted in his seat. "So the question is not whether someone can do check-in. The question is what level they can do it at."

"Yes," Jenna said. "That is exactly the question."

She handed out index cards and pens. "Now write down your task. Then define what novice, beginner, competent, proficient, and expert would actually look like for that task. Be specific."

They bent over their cards.

Pens moved. Pages turned. Theo crossed out his first version and started over. Lena paused often, thinking harder than she expected to. Caleb wrote fast, then slowed down when he reached proficient. Priya filled her card with neat, careful detail. Sofia used the smallest handwriting in the room. Marcus stared at the ladder for a long moment before he began.

When they finished, Jenna asked for volunteers.

Theo went first. He held up his card. "Front desk check-in. Novice needs the script and the sequence. Beginner can follow the process but misses details. Competent can handle a normal check-in alone.

Proficient can handle exceptions. Expert can teach it clearly and handle difficult situations without making the guest feel the strain."

"That's strong," Jenna said. "Clear. Practical."

Lena went next with the incident follow-up log. Caleb followed with morning gear prep. Each time, Jenna pushed for more specificity.

"What would a beginner still get wrong?"
"What would competence actually require?"
"What changes when someone becomes proficient?"

By the time Priya spoke, everyone was listening closely.

"Cross-team training consistency," she said. "Novice means someone only knows the version their own department taught them. Beginner means they can repeat their team's process but do not understand how it connects to other teams. Competent means they can perform the process consistently within their own department. Proficient means they can recognize where handoffs break down across departments. Expert means they can help standardize the teaching so different teams are not creating different versions of the same work."

Theo stopped tapping his pen. Marcus looked up from his notes.

"That," Jenna said, "is exactly why this matters."

She turned back to the board. "Now comes the harder question."

She drew a line down the middle of the board and wrote two headings:

> Assumed Level
>
> Actual Level

Then she faced them again. "For the task you chose, where have you been assuming your staff were on the ladder? And where are they actually?"

Sofia looked from the board to her notes before anyone responded.

Then Sofia spoke first. "I've been assuming competent when most people are still beginners."

Lena nodded slowly. "Same. Maybe worse. I've been treating some new staff like they should already be proficient."

Theo rubbed a hand over his face. "I've been calling people sloppy when really they were still at beginner."

Caleb looked down at his card, then back at the board. "I've been expecting judgment before people had consistency."

Marcus stared at the ladder, jaw tight. "I've been coaching people like they were competent when some of them are still novices."

Jenna let that sit for a moment. Then she said, "This is the real issue. Not whether people care. Not whether they are trying. The issue is that we have not been accurate about where they are. And if we are not accurate about where they are, we will not be accurate about what they need."

No one rushed to answer.

Marcus leaned back in his chair, arms still crossed. "Okay," he said, "but people still need initiative. We cannot lower the standard every time someone struggles."

"We are not lowering the standard," Jenna said. "We are getting more precise about how people reach it."

Lena nodded. "That matters. There is a difference between saying someone is not there yet and saying it does not matter whether they ever get there."

Theo pointed toward the ladder. "And this explains why some feedback works and some does not. If I correct someone like they should already be proficient, but they are really still beginners, I am not helping. I am just frustrating them."

Priya folded her hands on the table. "And frustrating yourself."

A few people smiled at that.

Caleb looked at the board again. "So if somebody is a novice, the answer is not more pressure. It is more structure."

"Yes," Jenna said. "And if somebody is competent, the answer may not be more structure. It may be more judgment, more repetition, more opportunity to adapt. Different levels need different kinds of support."

Marcus's expression shifted, not convinced yet, but thinking. "So what you are really saying is that we keep coaching the wrong problem."

"That is exactly what I am saying," Jenna replied.

After a brief silence, Jenna turned toward Priya.

"Priya," she said, "would you share that story you mentioned to me last night? The one from the Great Sand Dunes."

Priya looked surprised for a second, then nodded. "Sure."

She sat up a little straighter and took a breath. "Last summer I went to the Great Sand Dunes. I had seen pictures, so I thought I knew what to expect. It looked simple. Sand, slope, sky. I assumed it would be tiring, but straightforward."

She gave a small laugh. "It was not straightforward."

Theo smiled. Caleb leaned back and listened.

"I started up what looked like a manageable slope. Within a few steps, I realized I was working a lot harder than I expected. My feet kept sliding backward. I was putting in effort, but I was not making consistent progress."

She looked down at her hands for a moment, remembering.

"I kept asking myself what was wrong. Was I out of shape? Was I just tired? But that was not the problem. The problem was that I did not know how to move on sand."

Marcus uncrossed his arms.

Priya continued. "Then I saw a kid go past me. Maybe nine or ten years old. He was not stronger than I was. He was not in better shape than I was. He just understood the technique better. He leaned differently. He shortened his steps. He kept a rhythm that worked with the surface instead of fighting it."

Jenna nodded but did not interrupt.

"That changed how I thought about it," Priya said. "My effort was real. But effort was not enough. I needed a different method."

Theo looked from Priya to the ladder on the board. "So in that situation, you were not failing. You were just new."

"Exactly," Priya said. "I was a novice on that terrain. But I was judging myself like I should already be competent."

Lena sat back slowly. "That is what we do to staff all the time."

Priya nodded. "Yes. And when people are still new, but we talk to them like they should already know how to adjust, they do not just feel corrected. They feel inadequate."

Caleb rubbed his chin. "And if they keep doing it wrong long enough, they build the wrong habit."

"Yes," Priya said. "Then we come in later and act surprised."

Jenna stepped back toward the whiteboard. "That is why this matters. Skill readiness is not about labeling people. It is about identifying the level accurately enough to respond well."

She picked up the marker again and wrote a new heading beside the ladder:

Next Step

Then she turned back to the group.

"If we stopped here, we would have insight," she said. "But insight is not enough. So let's keep going. I want each of you to take the same task and answer one more question. What would help someone move from one level to the next?"

She pointed to Theo first. "Go back to front desk check-in. What moves a novice to beginner?"

Theo answered more quickly this time. "A script. A clear sequence. Watching someone do it correctly. Then trying it with support."

Jenna wrote as he spoke.

Novice to Beginner

- Clear steps
- Demonstration
- Supported practice

She looked at Lena. "Incident follow-up log. What moves a beginner to competent?"

Lena thought for a moment. "Repetition. The same form every time. A standard process. Maybe a real example to work from so they can compare what they are doing."

Jenna added it to the board.

Beginner to Competent

- Repeatable process
- Standard tools
- Examples and correction

"Good," Jenna said. Then she turned to Caleb. "Morning gear prep. What moves competent to proficient?"

Caleb looked at his card. "Normal days are not the problem. It is when something changes. Missing gear. A last-minute swap. A weather issue. So to move someone higher, they need practice dealing with variation. Not just the standard routine."

Theo nodded. "That's good."

Jenna wrote again.

Competent to Proficient

- Pattern recognition
- Variation
- Decision-making under changing conditions

She faced the group. "Do you see the pattern? Every level needs something different. You cannot move a novice with the same method you use for someone who is already competent."

Sofia had been writing quietly the whole time. Now she looked up.

"So the question is not just where they are," she said. "The question is what kind of support matches that level."

"Yes," Jenna said. "Exactly."

Marcus looked at the ladder again, then at his own notes. "For logging leads, I think some people are still beginners, but I have been treating them like they should already be competent. I correct the mistakes, but I have not defined the process clearly enough."

Priya glanced at him, then back at her notebook. "That lines up with what I have seen."

Marcus gave a short nod. "I know."

Lena reread what she had written and underlined one phrase. No one looked defensive. They were comparing what they had assumed with what they were now seeing.

Then Jenna said, "Let's test this in another way. I want a few volunteers to teach a task again. Only this time, teach it for the level the person is actually on, not the level you wish they were on."

Theo laughed once. "That is a little humbling."

"It should be," Jenna said.

He went first.

"How to check in a guest," he said. "If the person is a novice, step one is greet the guest and confirm the name. Step two is check the waiver. Step three is pull up the reservation. Step four is confirm trip details. Step five is direct them to the next stop."

He stopped and looked around. "That is already clearer."

"Why?" Jenna asked.

"Because I stopped skipping the basics."

Lena went next. Her second explanation of the incident follow-up log was slower and more organized than the first. She named the location of the binder, the correct form, and the first decision point. When she finished, she gave a small, embarrassed laugh.

"That was better," she admitted.

Caleb followed. This time, when he explained morning gear prep, he separated setup from decision-making. He described what a new person needed to do in sequence and what should wait until later training.

Jenna nodded as he spoke. "That is the difference," she said when he finished. "You are no longer teaching from your level. You are teaching from theirs."

Priya spoke next without being asked. "I think that is the part we miss. We teach from familiarity. Not from the learner's actual starting point."

Sofia looked up at that. "That should probably be written down."

Jenna smiled. "It should."

She turned back to the board and wrote:

> Teach from their starting point, not your familiarity.

No one argued with it.

Then she drew another line under the ladder and faced them again.

"I want to go one step further," she said. "Take the task you chose and identify one real group of staff. Not staff in general. A real group. New guides. Front desk hires. Seasonal team members. Whoever fits the task. Then write down their current level and one concrete next step."

The group bent over their notes again.

For several minutes, the only sound in the room was pens moving across paper and the occasional turn of a page.

Theo went first when Jenna asked for examples.

"New front desk hires," he said. "Current level: novice to beginner. Next step: standardize the check-in script and train from one version only."

Jenna nodded. "Good. Clear and usable."

Lena looked down at her notes. "New guest services coordinators. Current level: beginner. Next step: create one incident follow-up walkthrough and have them practice it with a real example."

Caleb followed. "Early-season gear crew. Current level: beginner. Next step: practice morning setup with live correction for the first week instead of assuming they will pick it up by watching."

Priya spoke after him. "Cross-trained seasonal staff. Current level: beginner across handoffs between departments. Next step: define the handoff steps and use the same language across teams."

Marcus took longer, but when he finally spoke, his answer was more specific than Jenna expected.

"New sales support staff. Current level: beginner. Next step: define what a correctly logged lead looks like, give them three examples, and review the first ten entries before assuming they have it."

Theo gave him a look. "That sounds like a plan."

Marcus shrugged. "It is more useful than being irritated."

A few people laughed, including Jenna.

Sofia was last. "Part-time administrative support. Current level: competent with normal data entry, beginner when exceptions show up. Next step: create examples of exception cases so they can practice making the right judgment before it happens live."

Jenna set the marker down and looked at the board.

The board no longer held broad complaints. It now showed staff groups, current levels, and specific next steps.

"That," she said, "is what I want you to see. Once you identify the level accurately, the conversation changes. You stop talking in generalities. You stop calling people lazy, careless, or unmotivated when the real issue is that they are still learning or they were taught inconsistently."

Theo leaned back in his chair. "It also makes accountability cleaner."

Marcus gave him a look. "I was thinking the same thing."

Jenna smiled. "It should. Skill readiness does not remove accountability. It makes accountability more precise."

Caleb stood and walked closer to the board. "This is the first time this has felt manageable," he said.

Jenna looked at him. "Why?"

"Because now I can see the difference between a person problem and a training problem. Before, it all got lumped together."

Lena nodded. "Same. I was reacting to the frustration, not diagnosing the level."

Priya closed her notebook. "And once you diagnose the level, you can stop taking the mistakes so personally."

Jenna stepped back toward the hearth. She had not expected the morning to become this specific this quickly, but she was glad it had.

They were not finished. Not even close. But they were no longer arguing about effort or attitude. They were identifying levels, gaps, and next steps.

"Here is the part I want you to remember," she said softly. "Skill readiness is not about deciding whether someone is good or bad at the work. It is about identifying their current level accurately, then helping them move to the next one on purpose."

Lena raised a hand slightly. "So how often do we do this?"

Jenna smiled. "Often enough that we stop being surprised by where people really are."

That drew a few quiet laughs.

Then she added, "And often enough that we stop assuming effort can replace instruction."

Caleb looked down at his notes again. The work ahead still looked demanding, but he could now see where to start. That was better than the frustration he had been carrying for months.

He wrote one sentence at the bottom of his page and underlined it twice.

Identify the level. Teach the next step.

When he set his pen down, he looked back at the ladder.

That was leadership, he thought. Not expecting people to catch up on their own. Not assuming that repetition meant mastery. Knowing where they were, being honest about what they still needed, and building the path one level at a time.

By the time they stepped away from the whiteboard, the afternoon light had softened. Outside the windows, the pines moved slowly in the wind.

No one rushed to pack up. They drifted toward the fireplace instead and took their usual seats around the stone hearth.

The fire crackled low. Jenna settled into one of the leather chairs but let the quiet sit for a moment before speaking.

Theo broke it first.

"You know," he said, staring into the embers, "I have spent years correcting the same mistakes over and over. I always thought people were not paying attention. I did not realize how often they were working from partial instruction."

Lena nodded. "I can think of several times I was frustrated with someone's follow-through, and now I can see I never clearly defined what good looked like at their level."

Caleb leaned forward, elbows on his knees. "I have been expecting judgment before consistency. That is on me."

Marcus did not speak right away, but when he finally did, his voice was quieter than usual.

"I push hard for results," he said. "I still believe in that. I can also see now that I have been coaching effort when I should have been looking more closely at whether people had what they needed to do the job well."

Sofia looked toward the ladder still visible on the board. "We have been measuring people against levels we never defined."

"That is exactly right," Jenna said.

Around the room, shoulders lowered. No one looked defensive now. They looked thoughtful.

"Today was not about lowering standards," Jenna said. "It was about getting accurate. If we are accurate about level, we can be accurate about support, correction, and expectation."

Priya nodded. "And that makes improvement more likely."

Jenna looked around the circle. "Tomorrow we start reworking our systems. But this is the shift I wanted today. Not blame. Not excuses. Clearer judgment."

Outside, the last of the daylight slipped behind the ridge, leaving the lake in deep blue shadow. Inside, the team sat in a calm, steady quiet.

They had more work ahead. Everyone knew that. But now they had language for the problem, a way to assess it, and a clearer idea of what to do next.

What This Means in Practice

- If performance improves only with experience, the required skills are not fully developed or transferred.
- If errors repeat, the skill has not been built to the level the work requires.
- If people rely on others to complete or check their work, readiness is uneven.

Apply This to Your Team

- What specific skills are required to perform this work successfully?
- Where are people relying on experience instead of demonstrated capability?
- What would fully prepared performance look like at the individual level?

These questions help clarify where your team is today and what it will take to move forward.

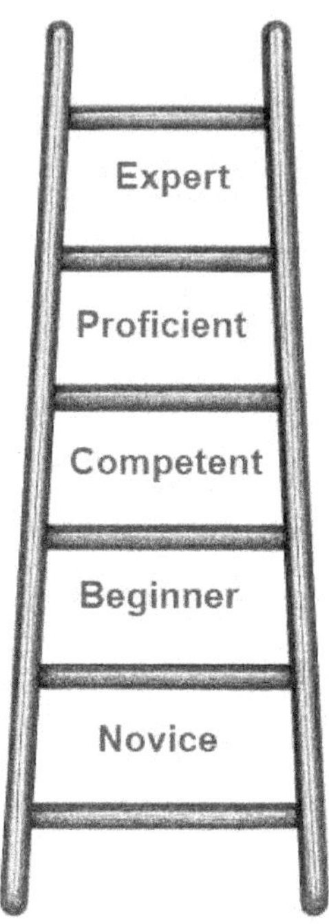

Chapter 5: Unspoken Rules

"Culture eats strategy for breakfast."

– Peter Drucker

The shuttle slowed as it pulled into the Mineral Belt Trailhead, tires crunching over gravel. Inside, the mood had already shifted. Packs were lifted from the aisle. Jackets zipped. Someone laughed about forgetting sunscreen at this altitude. Marcus leaned across the seat, pointing toward the ridgeline as he guessed what the day might hold. Theo asked whether a hike this long still counted as work.

"It does if we're learning," Priya said, smiling.

Lena nodded. "I forgot how much better my head feels up here."

The door folded open and cold air rushed in, crisp and immediate. One by one, they stepped down onto the gravel, conversation continuing as they adjusted straps and passed coffee cups back to the driver.

Jenna stepped down last. She waited until the group gathered naturally, boots planted, shoulders settling under the weight of their packs. Behind her, the Mineral Belt Trail stretched wide and gentle at the trailhead. The sky was a hard blue. Mount Elbert stood clear in the distance, its upper ridges already catching the sun.

"Before we start," Jenna said, raising her voice just enough to gather their attention, "this loop is a little over six miles. With stops, we are looking at three to four hours. Some sections are exposed, and there is moderate avalanche risk in a few areas."

That quieted them.

"We are well within our skill range," she continued. "This is not a casual walk. Pace matters. Awareness matters. We finish together."

Caleb nodded, already studying the terrain ahead.

"This is also not a hike to prove anything," Jenna said. "It is a hike to notice things. How we move. How we make decisions. What we assume without saying out loud. If something feels off, say it. If you need to slow down, slow down. If you notice yourself adjusting without knowing why, pay attention to that too."

Marcus grinned. "So no heroics."

"No heroics," Jenna said. "And no disappearing acts."

A few smiles moved through the group, and then they started out.

At first, the trail carried them easily. Boots found packed gravel dusted with frost. Conversation stayed light. Theo pointed out remnants of old rail beds. Priya asked about the history of the mining operations. Marcus and Caleb settled near the front, talking through their upcoming weekend plans and unfinished work thoughts.

Within the first mile, the shape of the group formed.

Caleb drifted forward without trying to lead. His stride was long and steady, the pace of someone used to moving with purpose. Marcus stayed close, animated and talkative, matching him without effort. Theo hung back just enough to watch the trail, the slope, and the tree line. Priya and Lena walked together, their conversation quieter.

Sofia walked behind them.

At first, she liked it there. From the back, she could see everyone. The spacing. The rhythm. The way people adjusted to one another without speaking. But as the grade shifted, subtle but persistent, she shortened her stride. Her breathing changed. The distance between her and the others grew by a step, then another.

She considered saying something. Not a complaint. Just an observation. The trail felt longer than it looked. The altitude was sharper than expected.

But the conversation ahead of her already had its rhythm. Laughter. Easy momentum. Forward motion.

A familiar calculation surfaced before she could stop it. If I speak, I interrupt. If I slow us down, I become the reason. If I adjust quietly, no one notices.

So she adjusted quietly.

No one told her to stay quiet, and no one had made her feel unwelcome. The decision happened faster than conscious thought. Her body complied before her mind finished explaining it.

Lena noticed.

They passed the remains of an old mining structure, timber half-collapsed and metal rusting into the ground. A faded sign marked it as historic. The trail curved around it without pause.

"Hard to believe people hauled ore out of here by hand," Theo said.

"Different kind of endurance," Caleb replied.

"Different rules," Marcus added.

The words hung in the air for a moment, then disappeared.

Later, as the trail narrowed near a stand of trees, a pair of runners approached from the opposite direction. Caleb stepped aside automatically. Marcus followed. The rest of the group fell into line without discussion.

Jenna, walking near the middle, watched the speed of adjustment, the absence of instruction, and the ease with which everyone complied. It was not chaos. It was coordination. And that was exactly the point.

By the time they reached a steeper stretch, the early energy had worn off. Breath found a rhythm. Packs creaked softly. The trail rose just enough to make effort accumulate.

Sofia felt it before she named it. Her calves tightened. Her breath grew shallow. Nothing dramatic. Nothing unsafe. Just enough to register.

Ahead of her, Marcus laughed at something Caleb said. The sound carried easily in the thin air.

Sofia knew what she could say. This section is steeper than it looks. We might want to tighten the spacing. But the group was moving well, and no one else seemed concerned. The thought came quickly: If this mattered, someone else would say it. If I say it now, I become the outlier.

She kept moving.

A few minutes later, the trail narrowed along a low ridge where patches of snow lingered in shadow. The footing had changed. It was no longer difficult, but it was less forgiving. Theo slowed first. He crouched, pressed the toe of his boot into the snow, and scraped back a thin layer to expose ice underneath.

"Hold up a second," he said. "This next section is slicker than it looks. One at a time through here. And if anyone wants traction, now is the moment."

The group stopped. Packs shifted. Breath clouded in the air.

Marcus glanced down at his boots. "I'm fine."

"Same," Caleb said.

Priya adjusted her straps. "I'm good."

Lena hesitated, then nodded. "I'm okay."

Sofia felt the moment stretch. She was not fine. Not in danger, but not fine. She could feel how much more effort it was taking to keep her footing steady.

Jenna's words from the trailhead came back to her. If something feels off, say it.

She also felt the pull of the group. Everyone else had answered quickly. Confidently. The group was ready to keep moving.

Theo looked at her. "Sofia?"

Every face turned.

The question was neutral, but it carried weight. Sofia felt heat rise in her chest.

"I'm fine," she said, matching the tone she had just heard from everyone else.

Theo held her gaze for a beat, then nodded. "Alright. Single file through here. Take your time."

They moved on.

Sofia stepped carefully and made it through without slipping. From the outside, nothing had happened. From the inside, something had been taught.

Lena walked just behind her and saw the tension in Sofia's shoulders. She saw the long exhale once they reached wider ground. No one had instructed Sofia to stay quiet. No one had told her not to ask for traction. But the rule had still been there.

Keep up. Do not be the exception. Do not make the group wait unless it is absolutely necessary.

Maybe not even then.

They walked another stretch in silence before the trail opened onto an old mining road. Wind moved steadily across the open ground, carrying the dry smell of stone and pine. Jenna slowed, letting the group bunch up.

Lena felt something click into place.

"Can I share something?" she asked.

Jenna stopped. The others turned.

"Of course," Jenna said.

Lena rested her hands on the straps of her pack. "When I first moved to Colorado, I joined a volunteer search-and-rescue group. I thought I knew what I was getting into. I had hiked. I was in shape. I cared about the work."

Theo nodded. He knew the type of group she meant.

"The first training hike I went on was a lot like this. Long day. Real terrain. Everyone experienced. Everyone capable. And everyone very quiet about what they needed."

The group leaned in.

"I remember struggling about halfway through. Not dangerously. Just struggling. My pack was not sitting right. My legs were burning. And I kept thinking, I should say something. Just ask for a short stop. But no one else did."

She looked down the trail behind them. "So I didn't. I watched how fast people moved when the trail narrowed. I watched who spoke and who stayed quiet. I watched what got laughed off and what got taken seriously."

Priya frowned. "Did anyone notice?"

"Not really," Lena said. "I finished. I didn't complain. From the outside, I looked fine. And that is how I learned the rule."

Caleb tilted his head. "Which was?"

"Do not be the one who needs something. Do not slow the group. Do not ask unless it is critical."

Sofia looked down at the trail, then back at the group.

"It was not malicious," Lena continued. "No one said it out loud. But everyone enforced it. With speed. With jokes. With how quickly we moved on."

She turned toward Sofia, not accusing, just honest. "What happened back there, that is how people learn culture. Not from a handbook. From moments like that."

Sofia did not answer, but her expression said enough.

Jenna nodded slowly. "That is peer norms. They are not what we say we value. They are what the group makes safe or unsafe in real time."

Caleb rubbed his jaw. "And once people learn them, they are hard to unlearn."

"Because they do not feel like rules," Lena said. "They just feel like reality."

They resumed walking, but the tone had changed. The trail still curved ahead in the same patient loop. The mountains had not moved. But now the group was watching itself more closely.

They returned to the lodge later than planned. Nothing had gone wrong. The trail had simply done what long trails always do. It stretched time. By the time they stepped back inside, the fire was lit and fresh coffee was waiting. Packs came off. Boots lined the wall beneath the hooks. The group settled into chairs with the steady fatigue that follows a full day outside.

Jenna waited until everyone was seated. Then she stood, uncapped a marker, and drew four columns on the whiteboard.

PRAISED
EYE-ROLLED
IGNORED
CORRECTED

"I want to make something visible," she said. "Not to judge it. Just to see it. These are not policies. These are reactions. What happens in real time, between people. When someone on your team does something, these are the responses they usually get. Not from leadership. From peers."

Theo leaned back. Caleb leaned forward, already reading the board like a map.

"Let's start with praised," Jenna said. "What behaviors do you see every week? No names."

"Covering a shift without being asked," Theo said.

Jenna wrote it down.

"Staying late to get a trip out," Marcus added.

"Fixing a problem without escalating it," Caleb said.

Lena nodded. None of it surprised her.

"Alright," Jenna said. "What gets eye-rolled?"

The pause lasted longer.

"Over-explaining," Marcus said.

"Double-checking something after a decision is already made," Theo added.

"Asking questions that slow things down," Lena said quietly.

Jenna wrote each one.

"What gets ignored?"

Priya answered carefully. "Pointing out small problems when everyone is busy."

"Or naming something inconvenient before it becomes urgent," Lena added.

"And corrected?" Jenna asked.

"Breaking flow," Caleb said.

"Making extra work for someone else," Marcus added.

"Slowing the group down," Theo said.

The board filled in. Nothing on it was dramatic. Nothing was cruel. But taken together, it was clear.

Jenna drew a line across the bottom and wrote: WHAT WE SAY WE WANT

"Now tell me what we say we value."

"Speaking up early," Lena said.

"Learning from mistakes," Priya added.

"Ownership," Marcus said.

"Safety-first thinking," Theo offered.

Jenna wrote each phrase carefully, then stepped back.

"Which of these are we quietly making unsafe?"

The room went still.

Caleb answered first. "We say we want people to speak up early. But we eye-roll questions that slow things down."

Theo nodded. "So they wait."

"And then we correct them for not saying something sooner," Lena added.

Marcus looked at the board. "We praise initiative, but only when it does not create friction."

Priya's eyes moved across the columns. "And we ignore early signals if they do not come with an easy fix. So people stop bringing us problems."

Sofia had not said a word. Her notebook sat open in her lap, untouched. Jenna let the silence stretch.

"This is not about blame," Jenna said finally. "Every culture does this. The question is whether we are aware of it."

Caleb rubbed his forehead. "So even when we say the right things, the group teaches something else."

"Yes," Jenna said. "Behavior learns faster than language."

Theo leaned forward. "That means our strongest performers are also our strongest teachers."

"Especially when they do not mean to be," Jenna said.

The fire popped softly. Outside, the light had faded behind the ridge.

Marcus shifted in his chair. "I understand the point," he said. "But we cannot pretend standards do not matter. Speed matters. Precision matters. Sometimes the right move is to keep going."

Caleb nodded slowly. "That is true."

Marcus continued. "Some of these norms exist for a reason. So how do we talk about this without sounding like we want everything slower and softer?"

Theo looked at him. "No one is arguing for lower standards. We are talking about the cost of teaching people to stay quiet."

"And speaking at the wrong time can have a cost too," Marcus said.

The room tightened. Lena felt it immediately. Two truths, both valid, pushing against each other.

Jenna did not rush to resolve it. "From an operations standpoint," she said to Caleb, "what happens when people stay quiet too long?"

"Late corrections," Caleb said after a moment. "Rework. Fixes that cost more because they happen later."

"And from a people standpoint?" Jenna asked, looking at Lena.

"Burnout," Lena said. "People blaming themselves for not knowing what they were never taught."

Marcus exhaled. "But we cannot coach every moment."

"No," Theo said. "But we can pay attention to which moments we shut down."

Jenna tapped the board. "Look at what we reward. Covering shifts. Staying late. Fixing problems quietly. These are outcomes. They show up after the fact."

Then she pointed to the second column. "Now look at what gets eye-rolled. Questions. Checks. Clarifying. That is the middle of the work. That is where people notice something early."

Marcus studied the board. "That is also the part that slows things down."

"Or makes things visible," Priya said.

Lena leaned forward. "And usually where mistakes get caught before they spread."

Caleb nodded slowly. "We do not penalize process on purpose. We just do not protect it."

The room fell quiet again.

"That is the problem," Jenna said. "Not standards. Not excellence. Where the pressure lives. We reward outcomes, and without meaning to, we penalize the process people need to get there."

Marcus sat back, thinking. "I do not want us to lose edge."

"You shouldn't," Jenna said. "Edge matters. But edge without trust cuts the wrong way. When people do not trust that it is safe to speak while things are still unfolding, the only time they speak is when the cost is already high."

Marcus looked back at the board, but this time he did not argue.

Caleb looked back at the board. “We have been relying on informal pressure to maintain standards. Speed. Expectation. Keeping up. That works until it doesn’t.”

“Because informal pressure does not just shape performance,” Lena said. “It shapes silence.”

Sofia looked down at her notebook and finally wrote.

Consistent responses shape future behavior.

She underlined the sentence.

Jenna let the room sit with that, then asked, “If we were designing our norms on purpose, what would we protect?”

No one answered right away. The question settled over them.

Then Sofia looked up.

“I think we are protecting the wrong thing,” she said.

Every head turned, but no one interrupted.

“We keep saying we want people to speak up early,” she continued. “But what we are actually protecting is momentum. We protect flow. We protect not slowing each other down.”

Marcus frowned. “Momentum is not a bad thing.”

“No,” Sofia said. “But it is not neutral either. When momentum is the most protected thing in the room, people learn very quickly what not to do. They do not interrupt. They do not question. They do not say, 'I'm not sure,' unless they are certain it is worth the cost."

Caleb nodded slowly. Lena's expression softened with recognition.

Sofia stood, notebook still in her hand. Her voice stayed calm and clear. "People are not staying quiet because they do not care. They are being rational. The group teaches them that slowing things down has consequences. Eye rolls. Corrections. Being seen as inefficient. So they wait. Or they say they are fine. Or they adapt quietly."

Theo leaned forward. "So what do we protect instead?"

Sofia answered without hesitation this time. "Early interruption."

The room stilled.

"Not constant interruption," she said. "Not chaos. But the kind that says, 'This might be small, but it matters.' The kind that catches things before they become expensive or dangerous or personal."

Marcus uncrossed his arms. "So instead of eliminating friction, we decide which friction we tolerate."

Sofia nodded. "On purpose."

Jenna picked up the marker and wrote beneath the board:

We protect early signals, even when they slow us down.

She turned back to the group. "That is not a slogan. That is a behavior-level commitment."

Theo nodded. “That means backing people when they speak early, even when it is awkward.”

“And resisting the urge to roll our eyes when it interrupts flow,” Lena added.

“It means correcting the process before the outcome,” Caleb said.

Marcus looked at the words on the board for a long moment, then nodded. “I can live with that. Speed still matters. Just not at the expense of trust.”

“Speed and trust are not opposites,” Jenna said. “Silence and trust are.”

The fire settled into a low, steady burn. For the first time that day, the quiet in the room felt like space instead of pressure.

Jenna capped the marker and looked around the circle.

“This is what peer norms really are,” she said. “Not what we put in a handbook. Not what we say in a meeting. Peer norms are what the group reinforces in real time. They are what people learn from each other about what is safe, what is respected, and what will cost them.”

No one spoke.

The board stood behind her, plain and undeniable.

Praised.
Eye-rolled.

Ignored.

Corrected.

And beneath it, the line they had chosen together:

We protect early signals, even when they slow us down.

Caleb looked at it and nodded once. “That changes the standard,” he said. “Not by lowering it. By catching things sooner.”

“By making it safer to be honest before a problem grows,” Lena added.

Theo leaned back in his chair. “It also changes what strength looks like.”

Marcus glanced at him. “How?”

Theo shrugged. “Maybe strength is not being the person who powers through everything. Maybe sometimes it is being the person who says, ‘Hold up. We need to look at this again.’”

Marcus let out a quiet breath and looked back at the board. “That’s harder than moving fast.”

“Yes,” Jenna said. “Because speed earns approval quickly. Slowing down to signal something early can feel risky. That is exactly why norms matter. They decide whether people trust the group enough to do it anyway.”

Sofia sat with her notebook open in her lap, no longer pretending to write. “So the real question is not whether we tell people to speak up,” she said. “It is whether our reactions make speaking up feel worth it.”

Jenna smiled. “Exactly.”

Priya looked from the board to the group. “And if we want a different culture, we have to react differently in the moment. Not later. Not when it is convenient.”

“That’s the work,” Jenna said.

The room stayed quiet after that, but it was a different kind of quiet than the one they had carried earlier in the day. It was no longer the silence of people adapting. It was the silence of people recognizing something true.

They had not solved everything.

But they had named the rule beneath the rule.

People did not learn culture from slogans. They learned it from each other. From pace. From reaction. From who got heard, who got dismissed, and what happened when someone interrupted the flow.

Jenna set the marker on the table.

“Today was not about fixing personalities,” she said. “It was about seeing the agreements you have been living inside. Some of them were chosen. Some of them were inherited. Some of them were never spoken at all.”

She glanced once more at the board.

“Now you know which ones are shaping you.”

No one rushed to respond.

Outside, the mountains held steady in the dark. Inside, the fire gave off a slow, even heat.

At last, Marcus stood and reached for his mug. "Well," he said, his voice quieter than usual, "I guess now we know what we've been teaching."

Theo gave a small, knowing smile. "Whether we meant to or not."

Lena looked at Sofia, then at the others. "At least now we can choose better."

Sofia closed her notebook and rested her hand on the cover.

The room stayed still. No one hurried past what had just been named.

For once, they did not choose momentum. They chose to notice.

What This Means in Practice

- If behavior varies across the team, the informal expectations are not consistent.
- If performance depends on who someone works with, peer influence is shaping outcomes.
- If undesirable behaviors persist, they are being tolerated or reinforced within the group.

Apply This to Your Team

- What behaviors are being reinforced by the team, even if unintentionally?
- Where do informal norms conflict with stated expectations?
- What behaviors would need to become standard for performance to improve?

Chapter 6: Breaking Point

"A wealth of information creates a poverty of attention."

– Herbert A. Simon

The lodge was slower to wake that morning.

Coffee was poured. Chairs filled gradually. People sat down more carefully than they had the day before, feeling the hike in their legs, shoulders, and backs. No one complained about it. They did not need to. The evidence was in the way mugs were refilled without asking, in the longer pause before anyone stood, and in the quieter rhythm of the room.

Outside, Twin Lakes sat still under the early light. The peaks beyond it looked unchanged. Inside, the group did not.

Jenna noticed the shift before she spoke. The people who usually filled space were quieter. Others seemed more at ease, as if the room's pace finally matched what they had been carrying. No one looked defeated. They simply looked like people recovering from real effort.

Someone broke the quiet with a half smile. "I'm still feeling yesterday more than I expected."

A few heads nodded.

Jenna looked around the table. "This feels different than yesterday," she said. Not as a question. As an observation.

No one disagreed.

"It makes sense," she added. "Yesterday asked more than we expected."

She let the sentence stand for a moment.

"This isn't about motivation," she said. "Or resilience. Or toughness."

She looked around the room again before saying the next word.

"It's about capacity."

The word stayed with them.

"For now," Jenna said, "I just want us to notice it."

The conversation did not stop after that. It changed shape.

People still spoke, but more selectively. Thoughts were finished instead of layered over one another. No one rushed to fill the gaps when the room went quiet. The quiet did not feel awkward. It felt earned.

Someone mentioned a stretch of the hike where the group adjusted without speaking, and the chatter faded as attention turned inward.

It was not disengagement. It was conservation.

Jenna listened for a while before speaking again. “I’ve seen that same shift at work,” she said. “Not all at once. Gradually.”

The meetings ended earlier, but not because everything had been resolved. Fewer people had the bandwidth to open one more difficult thread. She described teams that had once raised concerns quickly and now let smaller issues ride longer than they should.

“We usually call that a communication problem,” she said. “Or a confidence issue.” She paused. “But sometimes it isn’t either one.”

Theo leaned back, the question still on his face.

Lena had been quiet through most of the conversation, listening in the way she did when something was coming into focus.

“This reminds me of a place I worked in Winter Park,” she said finally.

The others turned toward her.

“It was an outfitter operation built around mountain biking season. From early morning through late afternoon, everything moved fast.

Rentals, trail support, safety briefings, gear checks, weather decisions. My role put me in the middle of all of it."

She described a workday built on constant adjustment. A shift covered here. A customer issue handled there. A trail concern managed quietly so the rest of the day could keep moving. Most of the decisions were small, she said, which was part of the problem. Each one made sense in the moment.

"On paper, it looked like a well-run place," Lena said. "People knew what they were doing. The days moved. Customers were taken care of."

She paused.

"But during peak season, the strain showed up the same way every time. Not in the morning. Later."

The room was quiet.

"Mornings ran fine," she said. "The checks were thorough. Questions got answered. The work looked sharp. By midafternoon, the edges softened. Not failures. Hesitations. Handoffs that needed to be clarified twice. A decision that took longer than it should have. Someone noticing a problem and choosing to handle it quietly instead of raising it because it seemed faster."

Theo nodded once.

"The strongest employees became the people everyone relied on," Lena continued. "They knew the gear. They knew the trails. They knew how to calm a frustrated customer or adjust when conditions changed. And because they could do it, we kept leaning on them."

She looked down at her coffee mug before continuing.

"They never said no. And we took that as proof they were fine."

No one interrupted.

"It took me too long to understand what I was seeing," Lena said. "We were managing the day well. We were not managing how much the same people were quietly carrying by the end of it."

The room stayed quiet after she finished.

Jenna nodded. "That's the mistake we keep making at work," she said. "We look at the task in front of someone and assume that tells us their capacity. It doesn't. Capacity is not just how much work people have. It is how much they are already carrying while they do it."

Caleb looked down at his notes. Theo stopped tapping his pen.

Jenna stood and moved to the whiteboard.

"We keep treating capacity like a headcount question," she said. "Sometimes it is. But just as often, it is a load question. What are people carrying that no one has counted?"

She uncapped a marker and wrote the first heading:

Task Load

"This is the visible work," she said. "Assignments. Coverage. Deliverables. Extra tasks people can point to."

Then she wrote:

Cognitive Load

"This is the mental work. Tracking details. Switching between issues. Remembering what is unresolved while trying to deal with what is right in front of you."

Next:

Emotional Load

"This is what people absorb from other people. Frustration. Tension. Reassurance. Smoothing things over so they don't spread."

Finally:

Coordination Load

"This is the work of holding the seams together. Following up. Bridging gaps. Clarifying handoffs. Making sure things don't fall through when no one clearly owns them."

She stepped back from the board.

"People rarely hit capacity because of only one of these," she said. "They hit it when several of them stack on the same person for long enough."

That drew a different kind of attention from the room. Not abstract agreement. Recognition.

Jenna looked back at the group. "Let's use the hike for a minute. Not as a metaphor. Just as evidence. What did you notice in yourselves yesterday that was not visible from the outside?"

Caleb answered first.

"I was tracking more than I realized," he said. "Pace. Footing. Time. Whether we were still moving the way I expected. None of it felt like a problem at first. It just kept adding up."

Jenna nodded and wrote beside Cognitive Load:

tracking / decision load.

Theo spoke next. "I stopped talking," he said. "Not because I was upset. I just didn't have the extra bandwidth to narrate what I was noticing."

Jenna wrote:

reduced bandwidth.

Lena added, "I started adjusting to other people without saying much. Slowing a little. Watching spacing. Paying attention to who looked steady and who didn't."

Jenna wrote:

monitoring others and silent adjustment.

Sofia looked down at the table once before speaking. "I kept doing math in my head. How much farther. How much water I had left. Whether I needed to say anything yet. I didn't say that out loud, but I was tracking it the whole time."

Jenna added:

internal calculations / self-management.

The room was still.

Then Jenna turned back toward them. “That’s shared capacity,” she said. “Not whether people are willing to keep going. Not whether they care. It’s what they are already carrying while they’re still trying to do the work in front of them.”

No one argued.

“At work,” she continued, “we usually see the task and miss the rest. We see the meeting. The customer issue. The report. The schedule change. What we often don’t see is everything else the person is already holding while they respond.”

Theo leaned back in his chair. “So we look at output and assume that tells us whether someone has room.”

“Yes,” Jenna said. “And sometimes it tells us very little.”

Sofia glanced back up at the board. “Because the visible work is only part of the load.”

“Exactly,” Jenna said.

She looked at Lena. “What you described in Winter Park is what makes this hard to catch. The work kept getting done.”

Lena nodded.

"And because the work kept getting done," Jenna continued, "the extra weight carried by the same people looked like reliability instead of overload."

Lena's pen paused above the page.

Caleb folded his arms. "We do that all the time. The strongest people become the shock absorbers."

Theo let out a breath through his nose. "And then we call them dependable."

"Which they are," Jenna said. "But that doesn't mean the load is sustainable."

Priya, who had been writing steadily for most of the conversation, looked up. "So when people stop speaking up, it may not mean they don't care. It may mean they don't have room to take on one more thread."

Jenna nodded. "Yes."

Silence held for a second.

Then Jenna said, "And that is where leaders misread the signal. We see less input, fewer questions, shorter responses, and we assume disengagement. But sometimes what we're seeing is saturation."

Around the table, people seemed to recognize the pattern at the same time.

It mattered because it named what they had all been sensing but had not yet said clearly.

Jenna sat back down, but left the board untouched.

"A few weeks ago," she said, "there was a meeting about next quarter's priorities. The timeline was tight. Everyone in the room knew it. I could see it on people's faces. But no one said it."

She paused.

"Afterward, three people came to me separately and named concerns they had not raised in the room. Fear was not the issue. They were already carrying too much to open one more difficult conversation in the moment."

No one moved.

"That's when I started realizing we were reading silence too simply," Jenna said.

Theo looked back at the board. "So if somebody looks quiet, we shouldn't jump straight to motivation."

"No," Jenna said. "Not until we've asked what kind of load they're under."

Caleb tapped one finger against his arm. "We keep asking whether people can handle the task. We should also be asking what else the system is asking them to absorb while they do it."

Jenna nodded once. "That's exactly the question."

The conversation paused there, not from uncertainty, but because the group was starting to see capacity differently.

After a moment, Priya spoke.

"This changes how I think about support," she said. "We usually respond to visible breakdown. We don't do much to identify load before it starts showing up in the work."

"That's because visible breakdown is easier to measure," Sofia said.

"True," Jenna replied. "But it's usually late."

Lena looked again at the four headings on the board. "Task. Cognitive. Emotional. Coordination."

She said the words slowly, as if testing the shape of them.

"That's a lot of invisible work," she said.

"It is," Jenna answered. "And when it keeps landing on the same people, shared capacity stops being shared."

Theo leaned forward. "So the question is not just whether the team has enough people. It's whether the load is actually distributed."

"Yes," Jenna said. "And whether the work design keeps creating extra load that no one has named."

Outside, a breeze moved across the lake. Inside, the room had become more focused, less diffuse. Not lighter. Clearer.

No one rushed to turn the conversation into a plan.

That, too, mattered.

This did not need a fix yet. It needed a better diagnosis.

Eventually, mugs were refilled. Someone stood to stretch. The morning moved forward, but the room did not go back to where it had started.

They could see the problem more accurately now.

The strongest people were not simply stepping up out of character or commitment. They were often carrying work the system had failed to distribute, define, or remove.

Silence was not always disengagement.

Sometimes it was the sound of too much already being held.

They had not solved the problem. But they had stopped misreading it.

Capacity was not about toughness.

It was about load, and too much of that load had been hidden in plain sight.

What This Means in Practice

- If priorities compete, capacity is not aligned with demand.
- If work is consistently delayed, there is more required than can be completed.
- If people are making tradeoffs without guidance, the system is relying on individual judgment instead of clear prioritization.

Apply This to Your Team

- What work is currently competing for the same time and attention?
- Where are people forced to choose what gets done and what does not?
- What would need to change to bring workload and capacity into alignment?

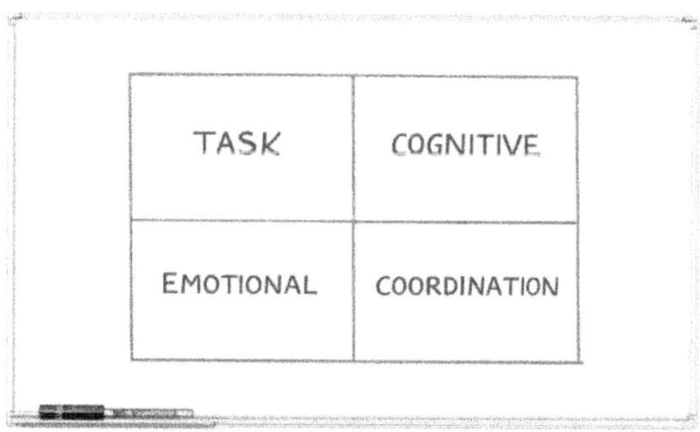

Chapter 7: The Wrong Signals

"Show me the incentives, and I'll show you the outcome."

– Charlie Munger

The lodge was quieter that morning, though not from exhaustion. The group had settled into the pace of the week. Coffee cups stayed on the table longer. Jackets remained draped over chair backs instead of being pulled on right away. Outside, Twin Lakes sat still under a pale sky.

No one was in a hurry.

Jenna stood near the window while the others gathered. The plan for the day was simple: a short drive and a walk, enough to get outside without turning the day into another long hike.

Marcus noticed the difference right away. "So this is more of a field trip?" he asked, glancing at the whiteboard where the day's outline had been written.

A few people smiled.

"Something like that," Jenna said. "Today is about paying attention to what surroundings teach people to trust. No one has to explain it. The environment keeps sending the same message."

That got their attention.

They moved toward the door in an unhurried way, boots thudding softly across the wood floor. Outside, the air was cold and clear. It sharpened the edges of everything.

The road climbed quickly once they left Twin Lakes. Trees thinned. Guardrails appeared more often. Snow still clung to patches of ground where the sun had not fully reached. Inside the shuttle, conversation came and went. Someone pointed out a ridgeline. Someone else commented on how quickly weather changed at this elevation. Phones appeared briefly, then disappeared again as service dropped away.

No one announced it. They simply adjusted.

The shuttle pulled into a gravel turnout near the crest of the pass. A cluster of interpretive signs stood just beyond the parking area. They were clean, official, and easy to read, with brown backgrounds, white lettering, and agency logos in the corners.

Jenna stepped aside and let the group spread out.

One sign explained the founding of Independence Ghost Town in the late nineteenth century. Another listed what had once stood there: hotels, boarding houses, saloons, general stores, a post office, a town council. A third described the population at its peak and the scale of the mining activity that had made the place seem viable.

"This wasn't some temporary camp," Sofia said as she read. "They planned this."

Theo nodded. "You don't build all that if you think you'll be gone in a year."

Marcus stayed a few steps back, hands in his pockets, reading without speaking. What struck him first was not the ambition. It was the certainty. The signs described the town as if the logic of building it there had once been obvious. Growth, permanence, and opportunity were built into the language.

Below them, the land sloped toward what remained of the town. From that vantage point, they could already see the outlines of foundations and the dark angles of a few structures that had stayed standing.

"This is farther down than I expected," Lena said. "You can't really see the whole thing from up here."

Jenna nodded. "That matters."

They stayed at the signs longer than anyone had planned. People read them twice. Someone traced a date carved into the edge of a panel. The wind picked up and pulled at jackets.

Then Jenna nodded toward the trail. "Let's go down."

The walk was short but steady. As they moved lower, the town became easier to read. Foundations marked where walls had stood. A few cabins still held their shape. Paths between buildings were visible in the ground. The layout was not random. Buildings faced each other. Distances between them made sense. The place had been designed to function.

Caleb slowed and took it in. "This was laid out intentionally."

He was right. Nothing about it looked improvised.

Marcus noticed how the paths curved, where doors would have opened, where people would have crossed one another during a normal day. He pictured the town when it was active: supplies stacked behind counters, smoke from stoves, people returning to the same places often enough that the layout became part of how they thought.

"This would have taken a lot of work," Theo said.

"And commitment," Lena added. "Once you build this much, leaving becomes a different kind of decision."

Marcus did not answer right away. He was looking at a wider foundation near the center of the town. It seemed to have been an important building. He imagined people orienting toward it, waiting for information there, measuring their own choices against what they heard inside it.

"This must have been a hub," Sofia said, joining him.

Marcus nodded. “Probably. You don’t build a place like this unless you expect people to keep showing up.”

The wind moved through the town and caught a loose board on one of the surviving structures. The sound was sharp and brief. Marcus looked back uphill toward the signs they had just left. From here, they were barely visible.

That changed something for him. Up above, the signs had made the place feel reasonable and established. Down here, standing inside the remains of it, he could still see the structure, but he could also see the distance between what people had believed and what the place could actually sustain.

He looked around again. “They didn’t stay because they were stubborn.”

Lena glanced at him. “No.”

“They stayed because everything around them told them staying was still the right call.”

That was the hinge.

Marcus felt the thought settle as he said it. The signs had done it. The buildings had done it. The money already spent had done it. The effort already invested had done it. The place had reinforced the same conclusion over and over: keep going. Stay longer. Trust what has already been built.

It was not a bad decision in every moment. It was a reinforced one.

Theo was reading from a plaque attached to one of the remaining structures. "Harsh winters. Supply problems. Lower ore quality. Competing towns became easier to reach."

"So it wasn't one thing," he said. "It got less workable over time."

"Without the environment making that obvious fast enough," Sofia added.

Marcus nodded once. "Exactly."

He could feel the parallel forming before he named it. Dashboards that stayed green. Meetings where speed mattered more than caution. Teams that praised momentum and quietly treated hesitation as drag. No one having to say the rule out loud because the environment made it clear.

A few steps away, Jenna watched him work it through and said nothing.

They regrouped near the middle of the town. Conversation had quieted. No one was looking at their phones. No one was in a hurry to move on.

Marcus took a breath. "I had a job like this once," he said.

The group turned toward him.

"It was in Colorado Springs," he continued. "Big regional operation. Fast growth. Clear targets. Numbers everywhere. I was responsible for partnerships and revenue, so speed mattered. Everything rewarded movement."

He could picture it as he spoke. The building. The parking lot already full before eight. Screens mounted on walls. Weekly meetings that started with metrics and ended with reminders to keep pushing.

"At first, it worked," he said. "Or at least it looked like it did."

The warning signs were small. A partner raising a concern after a meeting instead of in it. A contract moving faster than it should have. Questions that appeared in email later because they had not found room in the room.

"They were easy to dismiss," Marcus said. "Not because they didn't matter. Because the environment taught us what mattered most."

He looked down briefly at the ground beneath his boots.

"Speed got recognized. Confidence got recognized. Keeping things moving got recognized. Nobody told anyone not to ask harder questions. We just made it easier to be the person who moved things forward than the person who slowed things down."

Marcus kept his eyes on the ground while he finished the thought.

"I had people on my team who saw problems earlier than I did," Marcus said. "They knew where we were making assumptions. They knew where things were thinner than they looked. But they waited. Or they softened the question. Or they decided it wasn't worth interrupting the pace."

"At the time," he said, "I read that as alignment."

He let that sit.

"I thought silence meant we were on the same page. I thought if something was serious enough, someone would force it into the conversation." He shook his head once. "Now I think they were responding rationally to the cues around them."

The wind moved through the open space between the buildings.

"When things finally went wrong, it felt sudden," Marcus said. "But it wasn't sudden. We had built an environment where some concerns cost more to raise than to carry."

The group stood quietly. The town made the logic easier to see.

Jenna spoke then, her tone even. "That's what system cues do," she said. "They don't tell people how to do the work. They tell people what the environment is likely to reward, tolerate, or make expensive."

Marcus looked at her and nodded once.

Jenna continued. "Nothing you described sounds malicious. It sounds organized. It sounds productive. It sounds like people responding to what worked inside the system they were in."

Caleb folded his arms. "So when we ask why someone didn't say something sooner..."

Jenna finished the thought. "It's worth asking what they had learned it would cost them if they did."

Lena added, "Or what they gained by staying quiet."

"Yes," Jenna said. "Exactly."

She gestured lightly around them. "This place reinforced staying. The signs supported it. The structures supported it. The investment already made supported it. People did not need a speech. They were reading the environment."

Sofia looked back toward the path they had walked down. "And if the surroundings keep pointing in the same direction, changing course starts to feel irrational."

Marcus exhaled. "Even when it isn't."

Jenna nodded. "System cues shape behavior by making some choices feel practical and others feel costly. That is why they matter."

She looked at the group. "Let's head back up."

The climb out was steeper than the walk in had felt. The path did not look difficult from below, but leaving took more effort than arriving. Breathing shortened. Conversation dropped. People adjusted to the grade in their own way.

Theo stopped once and put his hands on his hips. "This is higher than it looked."

A few people nodded and kept moving.

Sofia spoke while still walking. "And leaving costs more than staying."

The group looked back at her.

She kept her eyes on the path. "That's part of it too. In most organizations, staying with the current direction costs less in the short term than changing course. You can keep moving without explaining yourself. You can stay quiet without standing out. You can wait and let momentum carry you."

She looked up then. "Changing direction usually requires someone to absorb the discomfort first."

No one corrected her. No one needed to.

By the time they reached the top, the signs were in front of them again, neat and official. The town below looked simpler from that distance than it had from inside it.

Caleb read part of one sign aloud. "Founded on the promise of opportunity."

"Opportunity feels different when you're tired," Theo said.

"And when changing course takes more out of you than continuing," Sofia added.

They climbed back into the shuttle and returned to the lodge in a quieter mood than they had left.

At lunch, plates were set out and coffee was refilled, but conversation took a few minutes to start again. Jenna waited until everyone had settled.

"I want to connect what we saw this morning to River & Ridge," she said. "Not the history. The pattern."

She looked around the table.

"At the ghost town, we saw a place where the environment kept reinforcing the same decision. The signs gave the place legitimacy. The layout made it feel established. The amount of work already invested made leaving feel expensive. Those were all cues. None of them told people what to do step by step. But together they kept pointing people in one direction."

Marcus nodded. Others did too.

"That happens at work too," Jenna said. "Not just through policies. Through what gets rewarded, what gets ignored, and what costs someone something."

She wrote three lines on the paper in front of her:

Rewarded
Ignored
Costly

Then she looked up. "When things get busy at River & Ridge, what gets rewarded?"

"Keeping customers moving," Theo said immediately.

"Handling things yourself," Lena added. "Not escalating unless you absolutely have to."

"Staying positive on the floor," Caleb said. "Even when something feels off."

Jenna nodded and wrote them down.

"What gets ignored?" she asked.

This time the pause was longer.

Sofia answered first. "Small concerns that don't force themselves into the moment."

"Problems without an immediate fix," Priya added.

"Questions that don't sound urgent enough," Lena said.

Jenna wrote each one.

"And what tends to cost someone something?"

Marcus answered this time. "Slowing momentum."

Theo added, "Raising a concern that turns into more work for other people."

"Being the one who interrupts when everyone else is trying to move," Sofia said.

Jenna looked at the page, then back at the group. "That's the point," she said. "System cues do not tell people how to perform the task. They tell people what the environment is likely to reward, tolerate, or make expensive."

No one spoke.

"So when we ask why someone didn't speak up sooner," Jenna continued, "we should also ask what the environment had already taught them about what happens when they do."

Theo leaned forward. "That means behavior is not really the starting point."

"No," Jenna said. "Behavior is the response."

She tapped the page once.

"If speed gets rewarded, people protect speed. If concerns get ignored, people stop bringing them. If speaking up costs credibility, time, or momentum, people learn to be selective."

Lena looked down at the three words Jenna had written. "Rewarded. Ignored. Costly."

She nodded slowly. "That's cleaner than calling it culture."

"It is culture," Jenna said. "But this is how you can read it."

The room stayed quiet for a few seconds while that settled.

Priya broke the silence. "So if we want different behavior, we have to change what the environment keeps teaching."

"Yes," Jenna said. "Not only what we say. What the surroundings, routines, and responses keep reinforcing."

Marcus sat back in his chair. "That's what I missed in Colorado Springs. I thought I was managing people. I was also reinforcing a signal."

Jenna nodded. "Most leaders are."

Lunch continued after that, but the conversation had changed. It was less abstract now. No one needed to be convinced that system cues mattered. They had seen them. They had felt them. They had named them in a way they could use.

By the time plates were cleared, the group had stopped talking about behavior as if it began with attitude or personality.

They were talking about what the environment had been teaching all along.

When people stood and drifted from the table, Marcus stayed seated for a moment longer.

He replayed the day in order: the signs at the top of the hill, the town below, the Colorado Springs meetings, the uphill walk back out, and Jenna's three words on the page.

Rewarded. Ignored. Costly.

None of it felt abstract anymore.

Sofia passed by on her way to the door and paused. "That town makes the point pretty clearly once you're standing in it."

Marcus nodded. "Yeah. It does."

Outside, the mountains looked the same as they had all morning.

Inside, the group was paying attention differently.

They would come back soon.

What This Means in Practice

- If people respond to urgency over importance, the system is signaling the wrong priorities.
- If behavior changes under pressure, cues are overriding stated expectations.
- If the environment rewards speed over accuracy (or vice versa), that signal will drive behavior.

Apply This to Your Team

- What is the environment currently signaling as most important?
- Where do those signals conflict with desired outcomes?
- What cues would need to change to guide more consistent performance?

Chapter 8: Harder Than It Looks

"To the man who only has a hammer, everything he encounters begins to look like a nail."

– Abraham Maslow

They reconvened after lunch. Plates had been cleared and chairs pushed back into place. Someone refilled the coffee pot even though most cups were still half full. The energy in the room had shifted since that morning. It was less reflective now and more focused. They had spent enough time at the ghost town for the conversation to move beyond history and back to work.

No one mentioned Independence directly at first. Instead, the comments came in sideways.

"Things don't usually fall apart all at once," Marcus said, leaning back in his chair. "They just stop working the way people expect them to."

Theo nodded. "You can usually tell when something used to work better than it does now."

Lena glanced out the window toward the lake, then back at the group. "People can be doing good work and still be relying on more interpretation than they should have to."

Caleb added, quieter, "And the more that happens, the more the work depends on whoever has been there longest."

That shifted the conversation. Instead of focusing on who was capable or who needed help, they started looking more closely at the work itself: what it required, what it assumed people already knew, and where the process was still leaving too much for people to figure out on their own.

Jenna let that shift happen before asking the question that would anchor the afternoon.

"Where does the work still feel harder than it should?"

Theo looked at the board first, then at Sofia. Then Theo leaned forward.

"Launch prep," he said. "Every morning."

A few heads lifted, and he continued.

"On paper, it's simple. Boats staged. Gear checked. Guests ready. Everyone knows what needs to happen. But if you actually watch it, it doesn't run the same way twice. One guide starts checking equipment immediately. Another waits, assuming someone else already did it. A newer guide stands close enough to help but not close enough to commit, watching for cues before stepping in. The veteran guides move quickly, adjust as they go, and catch gaps before anyone has to name them."

"It works," Marcus said. "Most days."

Theo nodded. "Because the experienced guides know what to look for."

Lena picked up on that. "They're scanning the whole time."

"Exactly," Theo said. "They're noticing what's missing, what hasn't been checked, and what could cause a problem later. The process does not make that obvious. Experienced guides have learned where it usually breaks down."

Caleb frowned slightly. "So when it goes smoothly, we assume the system is solid."

Priya shook her head. "We assume the people covering for it are."

Priya's comment changed the direction of the conversation. Someone mentioned how new guides asked the same questions during their first few weeks: where to stand, when to step in, what mattered most if things got rushed, and which checks could not be skipped.

"And once they've been around long enough," Lena said, "they stop asking."

Theo nodded. "Usually because they've learned the pattern, not because the work itself got clearer."

That was what they had all started to recognize across the week. The work was getting done, but too much of it still depended on people filling in what had not been made clear, visible, or consistent.

Jenna let the group sit with that before she asked the next question.

"If none of the experienced guides were here tomorrow, how would launch prep still get done correctly?"

She asked it plainly, like a real operational question. The room went quiet for a moment.

Marcus shifted in his chair. "It would still happen," he said. "It would just take longer."

Theo added, "And people would double-check everything. Which isn't bad."

"No," Jenna said. "It isn't. What would they be double-checking against?"

That changed the question.

"They'd talk it through," Caleb said. "Check each other."

Jenna looked at him. "And if they didn't agree?"

Marcus answered before he could stop himself. “They’d ask someone who’s done it before. Except those people wouldn’t be there.”

Lena said slowly, “So they’d be watching each other. Waiting to see who moved first. Looking for confirmation before acting.”

Jenna nodded. “So the work still happens, but only because people are paying extra attention to things the process should probably be helping them with.”

She gave the thought a second to settle, then asked one more question.

“If a capable new hire joined tomorrow, what would they still need to ask someone in order to do this right?”

The answers came quickly. Where to stand during launch. When to step in and when to wait. What mattered most if things got rushed. Which checks were non-negotiable.

Priya listened, then looked up.

“I think we’ve been calling this experience,” she said. “But a lot of what we’re describing is work the process fails to support.”

Theo nodded once. “That’s right.”

“When people stop asking,” Priya continued, “we tend to assume they learned the process. But sometimes what they learned was who to watch, when to move, and how to fill gaps quietly enough not to slow things down.”

“And because nothing breaks,” Theo said, “we call that a win.”

"Yes," Priya said. "But nothing breaking isn't the same as the process doing enough to support the work."

If launch prep still depended on certain people being present, then the process was not standing on its own. It was depending on attention, interpretation, and repetition to fill what had not been built into the work itself.

Priya sat quietly for a second before speaking again.

"This is reminding me of a job I had before River & Ridge," she said. "At Royal Gorge Bridge and Park. There were wind readings posted right where we worked, updated in real time. Everyone knew the closure threshold. If the wind speed reached that number, the bridge closed. The reading was visible to everyone, so no one had to rely on memory or make a judgment call in the moment."

She looked around the room.

"The decision didn't depend on memory or judgment in the moment. The threshold was already defined, and the reading was right in front of us."

Jenna nodded. "System cues teach people what matters," she said. "Tool support helps them do the work correctly in the moment."

Priya nodded back. "At the Gorge, no one had to stop and figure out what the rule was or who was supposed to decide. The information people needed was visible where the decision had to be made."

She connected it back to launch prep.

"That's what feels missing here. Too much still depends on who remembers the sequence, who notices the gap, or who has enough experience to know what usually gets missed."

"So this isn't just about training," Marcus said.

"No," Priya replied. "Training matters. But this is about what happens after training, when people are in the middle of real work. What does the process show them? What does it make clear? What still depends on memory, interpretation, or asking someone?"

Caleb leaned back slightly. "Documentation helps, but only if people can find it, stop what they're doing, and apply it correctly."

"Exactly," Priya said. "At the Gorge, the support was built into the work. You didn't have to leave the moment to go find the answer."

Theo rubbed a hand over his chin. "So the goal isn't to explain the work better every time. It's to reduce how much explanation the work keeps requiring."

"That's it," Jenna said.

More examples followed quickly. Handoffs that had to be explained every time. Judgment calls reconsidered because no one knew what had already been decided in advance. Routines that looked stable only when a specific person was on shift.

"It's not that we mind helping," Theo said. "It's that we've normalized how often the work still depends on being helped."

After a while, it became clear they were circling the same point from different angles. Jenna stood and walked to the whiteboard. She wrote two headings:

> Depends on People
> Built into the Process

Then she turned back to the group.

"Based on what we've been talking about, what currently depends on people?"

The answers came quickly, and she wrote each one exactly as it was said: remembering the order of checks, watching for what someone else might miss, knowing when weather really changes the plan, knowing who to ask, and knowing what matters most when time gets tight.

Then she tapped the second heading.

"If those same things were built into the process instead, what would be different?"

Theo answered first. "The information would be right where the decision happens."

"It would be visible," Lena added.

"And it would be defined in advance," Caleb said.

Priya nodded. "People would still need judgment. But they wouldn't have to build the structure from scratch every time."

Jenna wrote their phrases beneath the second heading:

Right where the decision happens
Visible
Defined in advance

Then she stepped back and let them study the contrast on the board. One side showed what people were still being asked to carry. The other showed what the process could have held for them instead.

“This is what tool support changes,” Jenna said. “It moves critical parts of the work out of people’s memory and into the process itself.”

The group looked from one side of the board to the other. They did not need to. The difference was visible now.

Caleb looked back at the board and said, “That means we’ve been calling some things judgment that are really just missing structure.”

“Yes,” Jenna said. “And that matters because judgment should be used for variation, not for filling the same predictable gaps every day.”

Marcus looked at the board. “So the issue isn’t whether people are capable. It’s how much the work still depends on capability alone.”

“Exactly,” Jenna said.

Lena folded her hands in front of her. “And if the process doesn’t carry enough of the work, the same people keep becoming the backup system.”

Theo gave a short nod. “That’s what launch prep has been.”

Sofia had been quiet, writing. Now she looked up.

"This also changes what consistency means," she said. "We tend to think consistency means trained people doing the work the same way. But real consistency comes when the work itself makes the right thing easier to do."

Caleb nodded once, as if the distinction finally had a place to go.

Jenna looked at the board again, then back at the group. "Yes," she said. "That's the point."

The room stayed quiet for a few seconds, not from uncertainty, but from recognition. They were no longer talking about whether people cared enough, remembered enough, or had enough experience. They were talking about whether the work itself was doing enough to support correct action in the moment.

By the time the conversation began to loosen, the pattern was clear. Launch prep was not unstable because people were careless. It was unstable because too much of the structure still depended on memory, experience, and informal correction. Priya's story had given them a contrast. The board had made the difference visible.

What the best employees had been carrying all along should not have needed to stay with them.

That was the work now.

What This Means in Practice

- If workarounds are common, the tools are not supporting the work effectively.
- If performance depends on individual systems or memory, the tools are insufficient.
- If tasks take longer than expected, friction exists in how the work is supported.

Apply This to Your Team

- What tools are required to complete this work effectively?
- Where are people compensating for tool limitations?
- What would need to change to make the work easier to perform correctly?

Chapter 9: From the Mountain to Monday

"You cannot change your destination overnight, but you can change your direction overnight."

– Jim Rohn

The lodge was quiet in a different way than it had been all week.

This was not the reflective stillness of early mornings or the tired calm that followed long days of conversation. This was the quiet that comes at the end of something shared and sustained. Bags were lined up near the door, packed with the efficiency that comes after several days together. Jackets were shrugged on and zipped as people moved through the room, checking travel times, and glancing at phones, already shifting out of the rhythm they had settled into here.

By the end of the week, they knew each other differently. They had spent enough time together to see one another more clearly. Fewer explanations were needed now. Less circling. More of the conversation moved straight to work.

The conversations were lighter now. Shorter, more practical. Someone mentioned the drive back to Boulder. Someone else checked the route home. There was an ease to it, but also a shared awareness that this week had required something from each of them.

Outside, the shuttle waited with its engine idling, ready to take them back down the mountain.

Jenna stood near the window, watching the light move across the lake. She did not gather them into a circle or gesture toward a whiteboard. There was no final exercise, no list of next steps written in marker. She waited until the room settled naturally, until people were standing with bags at their feet, ready to head out.

"Before you go," she said, "I want to thank you."

The room grew still.

"You gave this week your full attention," Jenna continued. "That is not a small thing. You stepped away from your teams, your families, your routines, and you showed up for something that does not always feel urgent, but shapes everything that follows."

She looked around the room.

"You did the work. You stayed in the tough conversations. You were honest about what is working and what is not. That kind of effort does not show up on a calendar, but it changes how an organization moves."

She paused, then added, "This was an investment in yourselves, in each other, and in the company."

There was no need to say more.

"You will head back into your normal roles now," Jenna said. "You will see your teams. You will see your systems. You will see the same pressures you left behind."

She did not frame it as a warning, just a fact.

"We will come back together next Friday," she continued. "Between now and then, pay attention to what you notice. What feels different. What does not. Where the work supports people, and where it quietly gets in the way."

A few nods. No questions.

"When we meet again," she said, "we will talk about what you saw."

The shuttle door opened, letting a rush of cold air move through the room.

They hugged where that felt natural. Handshakes where it did not. One by one, they stepped outside, the sound of bags loading and doors closing soft and unremarkable.

The shuttle pulled away from the lodge and followed the familiar road down the mountain.

The week was over.

The real test was just beginning.

By Monday morning, the rhythm returned.

Calendars filled quickly. Meetings stacked on top of one another. Notifications appeared the moment laptops opened. It did not feel abrupt. It felt familiar. The kind of familiarity that makes it easy to forget there had ever been another way of seeing the work.

This time though, they were watching it differently.

Caleb saw it before his second meeting of the day. A routine status update turned into a debate about a report no one trusted but everyone relied on. The workaround had become the process. He caught himself about to smooth it over, the way he always had, and stopped. Instead, he asked a quieter question. What would need to change so this did not depend on people compensating for it every week. He made a note. Not a solution yet, but a direction.

Lena felt it midweek, in a conversation that had the same shape it always did. Two people frustrated with each other, both convinced the other side was the problem. She listened, nodding, doing the quiet translation work she was known for. Halfway through, she realized how often the same behaviors were being tolerated simply because no one named them. She did not intervene at that moment. She started outlining what she would reinforce and what she would no longer absorb on behalf of the team.

Marcus noticed it in the numbers. Not the headline metrics, but the conversations around them. The pressure to move faster. The subtle shift from priorities to urgency. He heard himself using language he had questioned just days earlier and corrected it. Small changes in how he framed goals. Clearer signals about what actually mattered. He began sketching what needed to be said differently, and what could stop being said altogether.

Priya saw it in training requests that arrived already labeled as solutions. A new course. A new certification. A quick fix. She paused before responding. Instead of asking what to build, she asked what capability was missing and where experience had been mistaken for readiness. By the end of the week, she had a short list of gaps she was prepared to bring back to the group.

Theo felt it in the hallway. In the quick check-ins that were anything but quick. In the way small issues piled up quietly, carried by the same people over and over. He began tracking where the load was consistently falling and where it was never acknowledged. Not to rebalance everything, but to name one place where limits needed to be set.

Sofia noticed it in a spreadsheet she had opened dozens of times before. The numbers were the same. The story they were telling was not. Incentives pointed one way, expectations pointed another. She highlighted two signals that were teaching the wrong lesson and drafted a proposal for how one of them could change.

None of this was announced.

No one sent a summary email. No one rolled out a new initiative.

They worked the week as it was, gathering examples, testing language, shaping their thinking.

By Friday morning, they were ready to come back together. Not just with observations, but with points of view. With ideas grounded in real work. With levers in hand, not as theory, but as tools.

The mountain was behind them.

What mattered now was what they were prepared to change.

When they gathered again that Friday, it felt different than the retreat had.

They were back in a conference room. Familiar walls. Familiar chairs. Laptops closed, but within reach. The view outside the window was ordinary, and that was the point. This was not about creating distance from the work. This was about seeing it clearly.

Jenna watched them take their seats. There was less small talk this time. Less catching up. They had already done that work in their own ways during the week. What they brought with them now was quieter and more specific.

"I'm glad you're back," she began.

She did not recap the retreat day by day. They did not need a reminder of where they had been. Instead, she named what the week in between had been for.

"You went back into your teams. You stepped into the same meetings, the same systems, the same pressures. My hope was not that you would come back with answers," Jenna said. "It was that you would come back with clarity."

She let her eyes move around the room.

"Clarity about where the work supports people, and where it does not. Clarity about what feels aligned, and what quietly pulls against the outcomes you want."

She paused.

"Today is not about fixing everything. It is about choosing what you are willing to take responsibility for changing."

No one argued with that.

"You each took a different lens with you this week," Jenna continued. "You paid attention to different parts of the system. That is what makes this conversation matter."

She closed her notebook and set it aside.

"What I hope we do today," she said, "is put those perspectives next to each other. Not to debate them. Not to defend them. But to decide, together, what comes next."

She looked at the group, steady and calm.

"Let's start with what you noticed."

Caleb went first, not because he had the most to say, but because what he had noticed was concrete.

He talked about the meeting that had stuck with him all week. A routine status update. A familiar debate. A report everyone referenced and no one trusted. The conversation itself was not new. What was new was that he had finally stopped asking why people were making mistakes and started asking what the system was asking them to compensate for.

“We keep calling it execution,” he said, “but it isn’t. It’s workarounds.”

He described how much of his team’s effort went into remembering, translating, double-checking, and fixing things after the fact. Not because they were careless, but because the tools they were using required it.

“I realized how often I’ve relied on people to catch what the system misses,” Caleb continued. “We’ve treated that as professionalism. It’s not. It’s hidden labor.”

He was careful not to jump to solutions. He did not propose a new platform or a sweeping overhaul. Instead, he named one place where the work depended too heavily on individual vigilance. One process that only functioned because people knew where it broke.

“That’s the one I want to take responsibility for,” he said. “Not fixing everything. Just moving that piece out of people’s heads and into the work itself.”

Jenna nodded. Others did too. Priya nodded as if she had seen the same pattern in training. Theo looked down at his notes and underlined something.

It was clear what lever he was pulling, even without naming it.

This was not about efficiency. It was about respect for how work actually gets done.

Caleb finished simply. “If the process only works when experienced people fill the gaps,” he said, “then the structure is still incomplete.”

He leaned back in his chair, finished.

The room stayed quiet for a moment before Jenna spoke again.

Jenna nodded.

“That’s a clear place to start,” she said.

She turned toward Lena.

Lena spoke about a meeting she had been replaying in her head all week.

It was a standing cross-functional meeting, the kind meant to surface issues before they became problems. There were about ten people around the table. Halfway through the agenda, one person interrupted a colleague mid-sentence and redirected the conversation. The colleague stopped talking. No one commented on it. The meeting moved on.

Lena noticed it immediately.

She also noticed what she did next.

“I jumped in,” she said. “I summarized what I thought the person had been trying to say and redirected us back to the agenda.”

She paused.

"And everyone left feeling fine."

But that was the problem.

"When I do that," Lena continued, "I solve the discomfort in the room, but I don't address the behavior that caused it."

She explained what she had started to see clearly that week. The same people interrupted. The same people went quiet. And because she consistently smoothed the moment, no one else had to take responsibility for it.

"The message the group gets," she said, "is that interruptions are acceptable and silence is safer. No one says it out loud. The lesson comes from what keeps happening."

She looked around the room.

"That's a peer norm we've created. And I've been reinforcing it."

Lena was clear about what she planned to change.

"The next time that happens," she said, "I'm not going to translate or move us along. I'm going to stop the meeting and name what just occurred."

Not harshly. Not to call anyone out. Just clearly.

"I'll say something like, 'Hold on. I want to go back to what was being said,'" she explained. "Because if I don't, people learn very quickly that speaking up isn't worth it."

She leaned back in her chair.

"This isn't about being more confrontational," Lena said. "It's about being more honest about what we allow."

Sofia's pen stopped moving. Across the table, Marcus looked back at Lena instead of down at his phone.

They didn't need to.

The situation was clear. The pattern was clear. And so was the choice she was making.

Marcus did not start with a meeting. He started with a familiar number.

It was a metric his team reviewed every week. It was not the problem, the conversation around it was.

The discussion moved quickly. Questions were acknowledged, then bypassed. A concern raised by one team member was reframed as hesitation. The signal was subtle, but consistent. Keep things moving. Do not slow this down.

Marcus recognized it immediately.

"I've been unintentionally teaching urgency as a value," he said, "through repetition."

He explained how often speed had become shorthand for success. Fast responses. Fast decisions. Fast follow-through. Over time, the team had learned what earned approval.

"Fast equals valued," Marcus said. "And questions start to sound like friction."

No one pushed back. They had all seen it.

Marcus was careful to draw the line clearly.

"No metric told us to do this," he said. "We learned it from each other. From what got praised to what got waved through."

He shared a moment from earlier in the week. A team member had asked whether a potential deal was worth the tradeoffs it required. The question was reasonable. The timing was not convenient.

"In the past, I would have answered it with urgency," Marcus said. "Let's move. We'll figure it out later."

This time, he had stopped himself.

"I realized that question wasn't slowing us down," he said. "It was trying to slow us down enough to choose."

The distinction stayed with him for the rest of the week. He paid more attention to the language he used, what he reinforced, and what he dismissed without realizing it.

"I can't keep rewarding speed and then act surprised when people stop thinking," Marcus said. "If everything is urgent, nothing is clear."

He was explicit about what he planned to change.

"I'm going to name priorities more clearly," he said. "What matters most. What matters less. And when it's worth pausing to ask better questions."

This was not about becoming cautious or indecisive. It was about direction.

Marcus leaned back in his chair, finished.

Theo nodded slowly, but Marcus kept his eyes on the table. He seemed to be measuring the cost of what he had just admitted.

They were not talking about numbers anymore. They were talking about what those numbers had taught people to believe.

Priya began with a pattern she could not unsee.

"People are doing the same job," she said, "but they were taught it differently."

She explained what she had noticed during the week. The same role. The same expectations. But wildly different approaches depending on who had trained whom, when they had joined, or which manager they had learned under. Some people emphasized speed. Others emphasized precision. Some checked constantly for feedback. Others assumed silence meant approval.

"No one is wrong," Priya said. "They're just not aligned."

She described sitting in on a team huddle earlier that week. Two people presented work completed the same way they had been shown. One was praised. The other was corrected. Neither reaction was explained.

"They both walked away thinking they'd learned something," Priya said. "They learned opposite things."

Caleb leaned back and folded his arms, not defensive now, just thinking. Sofia wrote one line in the margin and circled it.

“What we keep calling performance issues,” she continued, “are often training and feedback issues. We assume shared understanding because the role is the same. But the preparation wasn’t.”

She explained how onboarding had shifted over time. How training had been shortened, adapted, or delegated. How feedback depended heavily on individual managers rather than shared standards.

“We’re asking people to meet the same bar,” Priya said, “without ever agreeing on what that bar actually is.”

She was clear about what she wanted to bring back to the group.

“I’m not talking about more training,” she said. “I’m talking about consistent training and feedback. One place where we get clear about what good looks like and make sure everyone is actually taught to do it.”

She closed her notebook.

“If people are guessing,” Priya added, “we shouldn’t be surprised when the results vary.”

This was not a motivation problem. It was a skill readiness problem.

Theo did not start with a meeting or a metric. He started with a pattern he could point to on a calendar.

“I keep seeing the same names,” he said.

He explained what he had noticed during the week back at work. The same people were being pulled into urgent conversations. The same people were staying late to close gaps. The same people were being copied on messages that technically belonged to the whole team, but practically landed on a few shoulders.

"They're the ones everyone trusts," Theo said. "So they get everything."

He described a moment from earlier in the week. A frontline issue surfaced late in the day. It was not a crisis. It did not require special authority. It just needed someone who knew how things actually worked. Three people were copied on the message. Only one responded.

"The same person who always does," Theo said.

That person was not assigned. They volunteered. They did not have extra capacity. They stepped in because they knew the work would stall otherwise.

Theo paused.

"This is what we keep missing," he said. "We think we're seeing individual effort. What we're really seeing is how the system distributes load."

He explained how certain people had become informal pressure valves. They remembered the exceptions. They handled the gray areas. They absorbed uncertainty so everyone else could stay focused on their own work.

"And because it looks voluntary," Theo continued, "we don't treat it like capacity. We treat it like character."

He shook his head slightly.

"That's not sustainable."

Theo was clear about what had changed for him. He stopped viewing these moments as isolated acts of helpfulness and started seeing them as a pattern the system depended on.

"This isn't about people working harder," he said. "It's about how much the system is quietly asking them to hold."

He named what he planned to bring back to the group. Not a full redistribution of work or a staffing overhaul.

"I want to find one part of the work where the same people are always the backup plan," Theo said. "And decide what we are going to change so that responsibility does not keep landing on them by default."

He leaned forward. "Shared capacity only exists if the load is actually shared," he said. "If it lives in a few people's heads and habits, it isn't capacity. It's an obligation."

Around the table, eyes dropped to notebooks and coffee cups. They all knew the names he was talking about.

Sofia waited until the room had quieted.

"I kept thinking about something Jenna said earlier," she said. "People pay attention to what helps them avoid problems."

A few heads turned.

"So I went back to the reports," she said. "Not to find a bad number. I wanted to understand what the system keeps putting in front of us."

She spoke calmly and precisely.

The issue was not that the team lacked data. They had plenty of it. The issue was that some measures were treated as operationally important and others were treated as background information. Both appeared on the report, but only a few consistently shaped discussion and decision-making.

"We say quality matters," Sofia said. "We say sustainability matters. But the measures we review most closely are the ones tied to pace, volume, and output."

She did not say it critically. She said it plainly.

"People respond to that," she added. "They learn very quickly which numbers require explanation and which ones do not."

That was what had shifted for her during the week. She had always thought of dashboards as tools for tracking performance. Now she saw more clearly that they also influenced performance by directing attention.

"The report is not only recording results," she said. "It is also showing people what the organization is paying closest attention to."

Marcus looked toward the window, then back at the report in front of him. Caleb gave a small nod, the kind that meant the point had become operational.

Sofia continued. "If one metric is always discussed first, reviewed most closely, and questioned most often, people will treat that metric as the priority. They will do that even when leaders say something else matters just as much."

She gave a simple example. A team could be told to make careful decisions, reduce rework, and protect long-term performance. But if the first question every week was about pace, people learned which result had to be protected first.

"No one has to say that directly," Sofia said. "The system is already making it clear."

She looked down briefly at her notebook, then back up.

"What I want to bring back is smaller than a full redesign," she said. "I want to identify one metric that currently carries too much weight in our review process and one measure we say we value but do not review with the same consistency."

She let the thought settle before continuing.

"If our reports and review routines keep emphasizing the wrong things," she said, "people will keep making reasonable decisions based on those cues."

She closed the notebook in front of her.

This was not about better intentions. It was about making the system cues clear and consistent so that people could see what mattered and respond accordingly.

Jenna let the room sit quietly for a moment.

She had listened carefully as each leader spoke. Not just to what they noticed, but to what they were willing to own. The places they had chosen to focus were different, but the direction was not.

"This is what alignment sounds like," she said.

She looked around the table.

"You didn't come back with the same answers," Jenna continued. "You came back with responsibility. Each of you saw the system from where you stand, and you named one place you're willing to change how it works."

She nodded toward the group.

"That tells me you have a real plan. Not a perfect one, and not a finished one, but a real one."

She was deliberate about what she did not say. There was no promise of quick results, no declaration that everything would be better in a few weeks.

"What matters now," Jenna said, "is that you test this in real conditions. Let the work respond. Notice what shifts and what resists."

She closed her notebook.

"I'm looking forward to seeing what this produces," she said. "Not just in outcomes, but in how the work feels for your teams."

She glanced at the calendar on the wall.

"We'll come back to this together at our next quarterly meeting," Jenna added. "That will be our moment to compare notes, see what held, notice what surprised you, and decide what needs attention next."

She stood, signaling the close without making a show of it.

"This isn't about getting it right," she said. "It's about staying responsible for the system you're shaping."

The leaders gathered their things, the conversation already shifting as they headed out.

They were not finished, but they were aligned.

Chapter 10: One Year Later

"There's no place like home."

– Dorothy Gale, *Wizard of Oz*

A year ago, Jenna had walked these blocks with a notebook hidden in her bag and a coffee sleeve already crowded with ink.

She remembered how the morning had felt thin and hurried, like the day had started before anyone had decided how the work would move. She remembered standing just inside the door, letting the store settle around her while she cataloged moments that were small on their own and exhausting in combination.

I just work here.
Wrong permit information corrected by a customer.
Excellence standing alone.

People looping between counters with no clear handoff.
A whiteboard issuing instructions that no longer applied.
A card reader that required patience, ritual, and luck.

None of it had been cruel. That was the problem. Everyone had been trying. The work had relied on individual effort to cover gaps that should have been designed out.

Jenna slowed as she approached the entrance now, letting those memories line up behind her. Not as judgment. As reference. She had learned not to rush this part. Change only shows itself when you give it space.

The bell over the door at River & Ridge Outfitters gave a clear jingle.

The shop settled around her. Pine wax. Coffee. The faint rubber-and-rain scent of shells drying near the door. Screens along the back wall still looped hikers on ridgelines, but the videos no longer felt out of step with the store. Above the entrance, the poster still read ADVENTURE STARTS HERE. The coupon that once covered the S was gone. Sun had softened the paper evenly.

Jenna stood still for a beat and let the place reveal itself.

She drifted toward the pack wall, fingers brushing nylon and webbing, posture loose, undecided. A staff member crossed the floor toward a couple who had slowed near the fitting riser. He did not wait for a question.

"Day pack?" he asked. "Long hike or city miles?"

The woman smiled, surprised to be met where she was. "Both, maybe."

"Then let's try two," he said. "Your shoulders will decide."

He walked with them, already adjusting straps as he talked. No glance back at the register. No hesitation.

At the counter, a short line advanced in steady increments. Conversation filled the gaps where waiting used to live. The card reader chirped once and complied. No ritual. No apology.

Near rentals, a whiteboard caught her eye.

> TODAY
> Staffing: Adjusted
> Returns: Front owns intake
> Trail Advisory: Updated 7:15 a.m.

The date was right. The handwriting varied. Someone had added a note in the corner:

> If it changes, change the board.

A year ago, she had brushed dust from that same board and found Monday issuing orders to Saturday. She had drawn a tiny battery with one bar left.

Now, the cues were current.

Near the rentals window, a customer hesitated with a return case balanced against her hip, scanning the signage as if bracing for instruction. Jenna felt herself slow, waiting for the familiar moment where good intentions turned into motion without direction.

It did not come.

A staff member on the floor caught the hesitation and stepped in. "Returns?" she asked.

"Yes. And we kept it an extra day," the customer said quickly, already apologizing.

"No problem," the staffer said. She glanced at the case, then toward rentals. "I'll walk it over."

At the window, the rentals associate nodded once and reached for the intake sheet clipped to the counter. "Extra day?" she asked, already scanning the barcode.

"That's right," the customer said, surprised to still be standing in the same place.

"Front owns payment," the associate said, turning slightly. "I'll mark the return. You're good to head up."

The floor staffer stayed just long enough to make sure the handoff landed, then peeled away without ceremony, already intercepting another question halfway down the aisle.

The customer paid once. The receipt printed. The case disappeared behind the counter.

No circling.
No calling for clarification.
No one explaining whose job it was.

Jenna stood a few feet back, unnoticed, and let the moment finish itself.

A year ago, this same exchange would have pulled three people into motion and still left the customer holding the weight. Someone would have been kind. Someone would have been embarrassed. No one would have been wrong.

Now, the handoff happened cleanly.

A huddle broke near the footwear wall. Not because time ran out, but because decisions had been made. Someone snapped a photo of the board before erasing it. Another person capped the marker and set it back in its place. The group dispersed without dragging the meeting with them.

Jenna moved deeper into the store.

The fitter stood at the pack wall, hands steady, voice calm. Her name tag was scuffed now, softened by use. She adjusted the teenager's hip belt and nodded once when the weight settled correctly. "There," she said. "That's your frame doing the work."

The kid straightened, surprised by his own balance.

"Take a lap," she added. "If it lies to you, we'll fix it."

Two feet away, another employee watched, then turned to the next customer and followed the same sequence. Not a performance. A pattern.

Jenna remembered the fitter from a year ago, brilliance flaring beside distraction, excellence unsupported by expectation. She had drawn a star next to the interaction and circled it twice.

Now, what the fitter knew showed up consistently, whether she was there or not.

At rentals, a couple approached with a hard case. The associate smiled, already reaching for the intake sheet clipped neatly to the handle. "Extra day?" she asked. "I've got it right here."

Jenna noticed that no one was interrupting, shifting, or pushing back the way they had before.

She passed the back corridor where the alley door had once stood open, voices drifting out while decisions stalled. The door was closed now, but not sealed. A printed schedule hung beside it, marked in pen. Someone had added a note: If you're in the canyon, check the board when you're back.

No policy speech. Just a fix that respected how people actually worked.

At the front, the senior guide leaned against the counter and listened as a customer described a route they wanted, though they were not yet ready to say so directly. He nodded and answered patiently. "Start at Fourth Street," he said quietly. "It's the same ridge, with fewer people. You'll know pretty quickly whether today is the right day for it."

The customer exhaled, relieved to be understood.

The senior guide glanced up and caught Jenna watching. Recognition settled into a small, knowing smile.

"Good to see you," he said.

"Looks like a good day," she replied.

"Most days are," he said. "Now."

She stepped aside to let a family pass and took one last slow scan of the room. People moved with less effort. They were not trying less hard. The work no longer required them to cover the same gaps by habit.

No one mentioned the retreat. No one named frameworks or levers. They did not have to. The improvements were now part of the normal routine.

As Jenna turned toward the door, she heard someone say, lightly, "Let's adjust it now instead of handing it off."

Another voice answered, "Yeah. That'll save time."

The bell rang behind her, clean and easy.

Outside, the day held that same high, clear light that makes plans feel possible. The Flatirons cut the sky the way they always had, patient and unimpressed by progress. Jenna paused on the sidewalk, hands in her pockets, and took a breath that felt different from the one she had taken there a year ago.

Back then, she had walked out carrying a list. Today, there was nothing she needed to capture.

She crossed the street and followed the side block toward the trailhead that cut up behind the neighborhoods, the one locals used when they wanted a long day without the crowds. At the corner, she stopped and checked the map board bolted to the post. Someone had updated it that morning. Conditions were clear. A note in the margin read:

Afternoon wind after two.

She smiled.

Jenna tightened the straps on the small pack she had brought with her, the kind you grab when you do not need much but still want to move. She stepped onto the dirt as it gave way from pavement to path, the sound of the city thinning behind her.

The work was steady now. It would keep.

Ahead, the trail climbed into light and stone, and her next decision. Jenna leaned into the grade and let herself enjoy the simple pleasure of forward motion, the kind that comes when the ground under your feet is solid and the direction is your own.

She did not look back.

Part Two
Applying the JL^3 Performance Levers™

Chapter 11: How to Use the JL³ Performance Levers™

Most leadership books assume the problem is motivation, mindset, or effort. This book does not.

The JL³ Performance Levers™ are designed to help leaders solve a different problem: results that fall short even when capable, committed people are doing their best work. When performance breaks down under those conditions, the issue is rarely character or intent. More often, the issue is the system in which the work is happening.

Part II of this book is designed to help you examine that system.

The six levers are not personality types, leadership styles, or phases of change. They describe the conditions under which people work. When one of those conditions is weak, performance suffers. When leaders misread the problem, they often push harder on people instead of changing the work around them. That creates pressure, not progress.

The six levers are:

- Mindset Alignment
- Skill Readiness
- Peer Norms
- Shared Capacity
- System Cues
- Tool Support

Each one shapes performance in a different way. None operates in isolation. In most situations, one lever is doing most of the damage, and a second may be reinforcing it. Rarely are all six broken at the same time. Your goal is not balance. Your goal is leverage.

This section is designed for practical use. You can move through it in order, but you do not have to.

If you are facing an active performance problem, begin with Chapter 12 to consider the issue from the perspective of an individual contributor, a team leader, or an executive. Then move to Chapter 13. The diagnostic will help you identify where the work is most likely breaking down. From there, go directly to the chapter for the lever that appears weakest. If a second lever seems to be reinforcing the problem, Chapter 20 will help you think more clearly about sequence and interaction before you act.

If you are not working on a live issue, read Part II straight through. That approach will help you build a broader understanding of how leadership decisions shape performance long before problems become obvious. It will also help you recognize why some interventions seem reasonable at first and still fail to hold.

Leaders are often surrounded by symptoms that feel urgent and persuasive. When quality drops, they are told to increase accountability. When confusion spreads, they are told to communicate more. When pressure rises, they are told to push for resilience. When adoption stalls, they are told to train harder or enforce compliance.

Those responses are common because they are familiar. They also allow leaders to feel decisive quickly.

But speed is not the same as accuracy.

A fast diagnosis that names the wrong problem does not save time. It creates a second problem on top of the first. Pressure rises. Frustration builds. People begin to feel blamed for conditions they did not create and do not control. Leaders become more certain that the people are the problem because the intervention did not work. In reality, the intervention failed because it was aimed at the wrong lever.

The JL^3 Performance Levers™ are designed to slow that rush to explanation. They redirect attention from people to conditions. They force leadership to ask what the work is actually asking people to absorb. They make it harder to confuse a symptom with a cause.

That discipline is uncomfortable at first because it removes some of the emotional convenience of blaming motivation, attitude, or communication. It asks a harder question instead:

What condition in this system is making good performance harder than it should be?

As you move through the chapters that follow, keep one principle in mind:

When the environment is poorly designed, strong performers can seem ineffective.

This model exists to help you see the difference.

Chapter 12: Applying the JL³ Performance Levers™

This chapter shows how to apply the JL³ Performance Levers™ from three different levels of responsibility: as an individual contributor, as a team leader, and at the organizational level. The levers themselves do not change, but the vantage point does. The conditions shaping performance are experienced differently depending on where you sit in the system. Start with the level closest to the problem you are trying to understand. From there, expand your view as needed. The goal is not to apply all three perspectives at once, but to use the one that gives you the clearest view of what the work is actually asking people to absorb.

Applying the JL³ Performance Levers™ as an Individual Contributor

Most people do not experience work as a set of systems. They experience it as a set of expectations.

Deadlines. Tasks. Priorities. Feedback. Pressure.

When something feels off, the first instinct is to look inward. Work harder. Pay closer attention. Improve communication. Stay more organized. Be more proactive.

Those responses feel responsible. They are also incomplete.

The JL^3 Performance Levers™ offer a different way to interpret what you are experiencing in your day-to-day work. They do not begin with the question, "What should I do differently?" They begin with a different question:

What is the work asking me to absorb right now?

That shift matters because many of the challenges individuals face at work are not the result of personal failure. They are the result of conditions that make good performance harder than it should be. When those conditions are unclear, inconsistent, or overloaded, individuals compensate. They fill gaps. They correct errors. They anticipate problems. They carry additional cognitive and emotional load to keep things moving.

From the outside, that effort often goes unnoticed. From the inside, it feels like strain.

This section is not about removing responsibility. It is about clarifying where responsibility ends and where conditions begin. As an individual contributor, you do not control the full system. You do, however, experience it directly. That position gives you access to signals that are often invisible to leaders.

The goal is to help you read those signals more clearly.

What it feels like when conditions are off

Most people do not describe system problems in structural language. They describe them as frustration.

They say:

- "This should not be this hard."
- "I keep fixing the same thing."
- "I'm doing everything I can, and it's still not working."
- "No matter what I do, something gets missed."

Those statements are not complaints. They are data.

They indicate that something in the work environment is requiring more effort than the task itself should demand. When that happens repeatedly, it is rarely random. It is usually tied to one or more of the performance levers.

For example:

- If expectations shift depending on who is asking, the issue may not be effort. It may be Mindset Alignment.
- If you are expected to perform a task without ever being shown what "good" looks like, the issue may not be motivation. It may be Skill Readiness.
- If the people around you are solving the same problem in different ways, and those differences create conflict or rework, the issue may not be communication. It may be Peer Norms.
- If a small group of people consistently catches errors, answers questions, or absorbs complexity for everyone else, the issue may not be teamwork. It may be Shared Capacity.

- If processes are unclear, inconsistent, or change without warning, the issue may not be attention to detail. It may be System Cues.
- If tools are difficult to use, unreliable, or poorly aligned to the task, the issue may not be competence. It may be Tool Support.

These distinctions matter because they change how you respond. Without them, it is easy to misdiagnose the situation and apply more effort where effort is not the constraint.

What people usually do instead

When something is not working, individuals tend to default to one of three responses.

1. Increase effort

Work longer. Double-check everything. Try to stay ahead.

This can stabilize performance temporarily. It does not address the underlying condition. Over time, it leads to fatigue and inconsistency.

2. Personalize the problem

Assume:

- "I need to be better at this."
- "I must be missing something."
- "Other people probably don't struggle with this."

This creates internal pressure without changing external conditions. It also makes it harder to raise concerns, because the problem feels personal instead of structural.

3. Work around the system

Create shortcuts. Build personal systems. Rely on memory or informal fixes.

This can be effective in the short term. It also makes the system more dependent on individual effort, which increases risk for everyone.

None of these responses are irrational. They are predictable. They are also limited.

The JL³ Performance Levers™ provide an alternative.

What to do instead

As an individual, your role is not to redesign the system. Your role is to see it clearly and respond in a way that reduces unnecessary strain.

This begins with observation.

Step 1: Notice where effort is disproportionate

Pay attention to tasks that:

- take longer than expected
- require repeated correction
- depend heavily on memory or informal knowledge

- change depending on who is involved

These are not just "hard parts of the job." They are signals.

Step 2: Name the likely condition

Instead of labeling the issue broadly ("this is frustrating," "communication is bad"), try to connect it to a specific lever.

Ask:

- Is this a clarity issue?
- Is this a consistency issue?
- Is this a skill issue?
- Is this a capacity issue?

You do not need to be perfect. You need to be directionally accurate.

Step 3: Adjust your response

Once you have a working hypothesis, you can change how you respond.

> If the issue is clarity, document what you are seeing and ask for specific confirmation.
>
> If the issue is consistency, look for patterns and surface them.
>
> If the issue is skill, identify what is missing and seek targeted input.

If the issue is capacity, be explicit about what cannot be absorbed without trade-offs.

These are not complaints. They are contributions. They make the work more visible.

Step 4: Reduce invisible work

One of the most common sources of strain is invisible work:

- catching errors quietly
- correcting inconsistencies without discussion
- adapting to changing expectations without acknowledgment

Over time, this creates a gap between how the work appears and how it actually functions.

Where appropriate, make that work visible.

Not by escalating every issue, but by naming patterns that affect outcomes.

Example: When effort is not the issue

Consider a team member responsible for preparing client reports.

The expectation is that reports are accurate, consistent, and delivered on time. The individual is capable and committed. Still, errors appear. Deadlines slip. The process feels unstable.

The initial response is to work harder. More time is spent reviewing data. More attention is given to formatting. Checklists are created.

Despite this, the same issues return.

Looking more closely, the individual notices:

- Data sources are updated at different times
- Instructions vary depending on who provides them
- Previous reports are not reliable references because formats change
- Questions are answered differently by different stakeholders

This is not primarily a motivation problem. It is a combination of System Cues and Peer Norms.

Once that is recognized, the response changes.

Instead of increasing effort alone, the individual begins to:

- document inconsistencies
- clarify expectations before starting work
- flag differences in guidance
- create a shared reference point for future reports

The work becomes more stable, not because the individual worked harder, but because the conditions became clearer.

Diagnostic questions for individuals

Use these to orient your thinking:

- Where does my work feel harder than it should be?
- What am I consistently compensating for?
- Where do expectations change depending on the person or situation?

- What do I rely on memory for that should be defined?
- Where do the same issues repeat, even after I try to fix them?
- Which lever feels most likely to explain what I'm experiencing?

You do not need perfect answers. You need better questions.

What to keep in mind

As an individual, your influence has limits. You are not responsible for fixing every condition. You are responsible for recognizing when conditions are shaping outcomes.

That awareness does two things.

First, it prevents unnecessary self-blame. Not every performance issue is a personal failure.

Second, it allows you to contribute more effectively. When you can name what is actually happening, you give leaders something concrete to work with.

Closing

The JL^3 Performance Levers™ are not just a leadership tool. They are a way of interpreting work.

They help you distinguish between:

- effort and structure
- behavior and condition
- symptom and cause

That distinction does not remove responsibility. It focuses it.

Instead of asking, "How do I try harder?" you begin to ask:

What is making this harder than it needs to be?

And what is the most useful thing I can do about it?

Applying the JL³ Performance Levers™ as a Team Leader

As a team leader, you sit in a different position than an individual contributor.

You are still close enough to the work to see how it actually happens. At the same time, you are responsible for results that depend on more than your own effort. You are accountable for the output of a group operating inside a shared set of conditions.

When performance breaks down at this level, it is rarely experienced as a single issue. It shows up as patterns.

- The same mistakes appear across multiple people
- Certain tasks require constant oversight
- Strong performers become bottlenecks
- New team members struggle to get up to speed
- Work quality varies depending on who completes it

These patterns are often interpreted as people problems.

Someone needs more accountability.
Someone needs more training.
Someone needs to communicate better.

Those responses feel actionable. They also tend to miss the underlying cause.

The JL^3 Performance Levers™ shift the focus from individual behavior to shared conditions. As a team leader, your role is not to push harder on people. Your role is to shape the environment in which your team operates so that good performance becomes more consistent and less dependent on individual effort.

What it looks like when team conditions are off

At the team level, performance issues are rarely isolated. They repeat.

You may notice:

- The same type of error appears in different places
- Team members ask similar questions again and again
- Work slows down when a specific person is unavailable
- Processes are followed differently depending on the situation
- Expectations are interpreted inconsistently

These are not random breakdowns. They are signals that the system is placing different demands on different people, even when the task is the same.

For example:

- If expectations are met only when someone is watching, but ignored when they are, the issue isn't accountability. It is Mindset Alignment.
- If new team members require extended ramp-up time and still struggle to perform independently, the issue is not motivation. It is Skill Readiness.
- If team members rely on informal agreements or personal preferences instead of shared standards, the issue is not communication. It is Peer Norms.
- If a small group of experienced employees consistently carries the most complex work, answers questions, and resolves issues, the issue is not dedication. It is Shared Capacity.
- If processes are unclear, frequently change, or are interpreted differently across the team, the issue is not compliance. It is System Cues.
- If tools slow the work down, require workarounds, or produce inconsistent outputs, the issue is not performance. It is Tool Support.

These distinctions matter because they determine where you act. Without them, it is easy to respond to visible behavior instead of the conditions shaping that behavior.

What leaders usually do instead

When performance issues appear across a team, leaders often default to responses that target people rather than conditions.

1. Increase oversight

More check-ins. More approvals. More reviews.

This can reduce visible errors in the short term. It also increases dependency. The team becomes more reliant on the leader to maintain quality, which limits scalability.

2. Push for accountability

Clarify expectations. Reinforce consequences. Emphasize ownership.

Accountability matters. When used as the primary response, it often assumes that expectations are already clear and consistent. When they are not, it creates pressure without improving performance.

3. Add more training

Schedule sessions. Share materials. reinforce key steps.

Training is effective when a skill gap exists. When the issue is inconsistency, unclear processes, or conflicting expectations, training adds information without resolving the underlying problem.

4. Increase communication

More meetings. More updates. More reminders.

Communication can help, but it does not replace structure. If the system itself is unclear, more communication often amplifies confusion rather than resolving it.

None of these responses are inherently wrong. They become ineffective when they are applied without diagnosing the condition that is actually driving the problem.

What to do instead

As a team leader, your advantage is proximity. You can see how work actually moves, where it slows down, and where it depends on specific individuals.

Your responsibility is to use that visibility to shape conditions deliberately.

Step 1: Look for patterns, not incidents

Individual mistakes happen. System problems repeat.

Instead of reacting to isolated issues, ask:

- Where does this happen more than once?
- Who is affected?
- Under what conditions does it appear?

Patterns point to levers. Incidents do not.

Step 2: Identify the primary constraint

In most situations, one lever is doing most of the damage.

Your goal is not to fix everything at once. It is to identify the condition that is placing the greatest strain on the system.

Ask:

- What is making good performance harder than it should be?
- What are people compensating for?
- Where does the work depend on interpretation instead of clarity?

Focus on the answer that explains the pattern, not just the most visible symptom.

Step 3: Change the condition, not just the behavior

Once you have identified the likely lever, act on the system.

- If the issue is Mindset Alignment, make expectations explicit and consistent.
- If the issue is Skill Readiness, define what good performance looks like and ensure it is actually taught.
- If the issue is Peer Norms, establish shared standards and reinforce them through the team, not just through individual feedback.
- If the issue is Shared Capacity, redistribute work, clarify ownership, or reduce dependency on specific individuals.
- If the issue is System Cues, stabilize processes, define steps clearly, and reduce variation.
- If the issue is Tool Support, improve the tools, simplify their use, or align them more closely with the task.

These actions do more than correct behavior. They change the environment in which behavior occurs.

Step 4: Reduce reliance on individual effort

One of the clearest signs of a weak system is when performance depends heavily on a few people.

- The person who "knows how to fix it"
- The person who catches errors before they matter
- The person everyone goes to for answers

These individuals often carry hidden load. They stabilize the system through effort.

Your role is to reduce that dependency by making the work itself more stable.

That may mean:

- documenting processes
- clarifying expectations
- distributing knowledge
- creating shared reference points

The goal is not to reduce performance. It is to make performance less fragile.

Step 5: Make the work visible

Leaders often make decisions based on outcomes without seeing the conditions that produced them.

As a team leader, you can close that gap.

Make visible:

- where work slows down
- where inconsistencies appear
- where extra effort is required to maintain quality

This is not about reporting problems. It is about providing accurate information so that better decisions can be made.

Example: When consistency is the real issue

Consider a team responsible for onboarding new clients.

The expectation is that each client receives a consistent experience. In practice, onboarding varies.

Some clients move through quickly. Others require rework. Some receive complete information. Others do not.

The initial response is to reinforce accountability.

- Review errors with individual team members
- Remind the team of expectations
- Increase oversight on new cases

Despite this, inconsistency continues.

Looking more closely, the leader notices:

- Different team members follow different steps
- There is no single reference for the onboarding process
- Questions are answered differently depending on who is asked
- Experienced team members adjust the process informally

This is not primarily an accountability issue. It is a combination of Peer Norms and System Cues.

Once that is recognized, the leader shifts focus.

Instead of increasing pressure on individuals, the leader:

- defines a clear, shared process
- creates a consistent reference point
- aligns expectations across the team
- reduces variation in how the work is performed

Consistency improves, not because individuals tried harder, but because the conditions supporting the work became stable.

Diagnostic questions for team leaders

Use these to guide your thinking:

- Where do the same problems appear across multiple people?
- What do my strongest performers compensate for that others cannot?
- Where does work depend on interpretation instead of clarity?
- What varies depending on who is doing the work?
- Where are we relying on informal knowledge instead of defined processes?
- Which lever best explains the patterns I am seeing?

These questions are not a checklist. They are a way of focusing attention on conditions rather than symptoms.

What to keep in mind

As a team leader, you are often the first level at which system issues become visible as patterns.

That position comes with a choice.

You can respond to those patterns as individual performance issues, or you can treat them as signals about the conditions shaping the work.

The first approach produces short-term corrections. The second produces more stable performance over time.

Closing

The JL^3 Performance Levers™ shift leadership from reaction to design.

They make it possible to move beyond:

- correcting errors
- reinforcing expectations
- increasing oversight

and toward:

- clarifying conditions
- stabilizing processes
- aligning the environment with the work

As a team leader, that shift is where your influence becomes most visible.

Not in how hard your team works, but in how consistently they can perform without unnecessary strain.

Applying the JL³ Performance Levers™ at the Organizational Level

At the executive level, performance is experienced through outcomes.

Metrics. Trends. Variability across teams. You do not see the day-to-day work directly. You see the results of it.

When those results shift, the instinct is to respond quickly.

- Set clearer expectations.
- Increase accountability.
- Launch new initiatives.
- Standardize through directive.

These actions feel decisive. They are often based on incomplete information.

The risk at this level is speed.

A fast response that targets the wrong problem does not save time. It creates a second problem on top of the first.

Outcomes tell you where to look. The levers tell you what to look for.

Your role is not to react to the numbers themselves. Your role is to use them as signals to direct attention to the work.

Using performance metrics to guide where to look

At the executive level, performance appears through a small set of metrics: financial results, output, quality, speed, customer outcomes, and workforce indicators.

These are lagging indicators. They tell you something changed. They do not tell you which condition caused it.

Some signals are straightforward. Others are complex and involve multiple conditions interacting.

Use the patterns in your metrics to narrow where to look first.

When quality declines

Most likely levers: System Cues, Skill Readiness

Also consider: Tool Support

Look for:

- unclear or inconsistent processes
- gaps in capability
- variation introduced by tools

When speed slows

Most likely levers: Shared Capacity, System Cues

Also consider: Tool Support

Look for:

- workload exceeding capacity
- delays in flow or handoffs
- unnecessary steps or variation

When output declines

Most likely levers: Shared Capacity, Tool Support

Also consider: Skill Readiness

Look for:

- constraints on time or resources
- friction in tools
- gaps in independent capability

When results vary across teams

Most likely levers: System Cues, Peer Norms

Also consider: Skill Readiness

Look for:

- differences in process or expectations
- lack of shared standards
- reliance on local interpretation

When adoption stalls

Most likely levers: Mindset Alignment, Tool Support

Also consider: System Cues

Look for:

- priorities not reinforced through decisions
- misalignment between processes and expectations
- tools that do not support the change

When customer metrics decline

Most likely levers: System Cues, Skill Readiness

Also consider: Shared Capacity

Look for:

- inconsistency in execution
- gaps in front-line readiness
- workload affecting service quality

When turnover increases

This is a multi-lever signal.

Most likely levers: Shared Capacity, Mindset Alignment, Peer Norms

Also consider: System Cues, Tool Support

Look for:

- unsustainable workload
- unclear or inconsistent expectations
- friction in the work environment

When performance improves but does not hold

This is a multi-lever signal.

Look for:

- one condition improved
- another condition continuing to reinforce the old pattern

Turning insight into direction

At this level, you are not adjusting the work directly. You are guiding others to examine it.

Once a pattern appears in the numbers, the next step is not to prescribe solutions. The next step is to direct your leaders where to look.

Instead of:

"We need to improve quality"

Say:

"We are seeing variation in quality. I want us to examine how the work is defined and executed before we make changes."

Set the expectation that leaders will:

- examine how the work is functioning
- identify the condition driving the issue
- recommend changes to the system

Support this by asking:

- What is making this harder than it should be?
- Where are people compensating?
- What is inconsistent across teams?
- Which lever best explains what you are seeing?

Closing

At this level, the quality of your direction determines the quality of the response.

If you direct attention to outcomes, leaders will react to outcomes. If you direct attention to conditions, leaders will examine the work.

That difference determines whether the problem is solved or repeated.

When conditions are aligned, performance becomes more predictable, more sustainable, and less dependent on constant intervention.

Chapter 13: The JL³ Performance Diagnostic

When results fall short, the most dangerous move a leader can make is guessing.

Most organizations respond to performance problems by pulling familiar levers harder. They communicate more. They train more. They add tools. They increase accountability. Sometimes that works. Often it does not, because the real constraint sits somewhere else in the system.

The purpose of this diagnostic is simple: to help you identify where performance is breaking down right now.

This is not a diagnostic about individuals. It is a diagnostic about work. Use it to assess a team, a function, a process, or a recurring result that is falling short. The goal is not a perfect score. The goal is insight you can act on.

Start by choosing one specific outcome. Not morale in general. Not leadership in general. One concrete result that matters and is not where it should be.

That outcome might be something like:

- missed deadlines in one department
- customer complaints about a specific handoff
- quality failures in one recurring step
- delayed decisions in a leadership team
- repeated rework in one workflow
- uneven performance across similar teams

The more specific the outcome, the more useful the diagnostic will be.

Once you have chosen the outcome, assess each lever by asking whether the system around that work currently provides:

- clear priorities and tradeoffs
- the skills required for current performance
- peer reinforcement of standards
- enough capacity for quality work
- cues that align with stated priorities
- tools that support the work instead of slowing it down

Answer based on observable reality, not intent. If you cannot point to evidence, do not assume the condition is strong.

How to Rate the Statements

For each statement, use this scale:

1 - Rarely true	2 - Sometimes true	3 - Consistently true
This condition is mostly absent or inconsistent. It may appear occasionally, but it does not reliably support performance.	This condition exists in some situations, teams, or moments, but not consistently enough to support dependable results.	This condition is clearly present and reliably supports the work as it is actually being done.

Rate each statement based on what people experience in practice, not what leaders intended, announced, or assumed would happen.

If you are unsure between two ratings, choose the lower one. A condition that only works sometimes is not yet strong enough to depend on.

If multiple people are completing the diagnostic, do not average away disagreement too quickly. Wide differences in scoring are useful information. They may signal inconsistent leadership, uneven conditions across teams, or confusion about how the work really operates.

After rating the statements for each lever:

- look for the lever with the lowest overall pattern
- then look for the second-lowest lever

- begin with the lever that appears to be creating the greatest constraint on performance

Do not use the scores to label a team as good or bad. Use them to identify where the work needs attention first.

The Diagnostic

Rate each statement 1, 2, or 3. For a printable worksheet and scoring guide, visit our website found in Companion Resources.

Mindset Alignment

Do people understand what success looks like and why it matters?

1. People can explain the primary objective of the work in similar terms.
2. Competing priorities are explicitly ranked when tradeoffs appear.
3. Leaders make consistent decisions when similar situations arise.

Skill Readiness

Do people have the capability required to perform the work as designed?

1. The skills required for current performance are clearly defined.
2. People have had a real opportunity to learn and practice those skills.

3. Quality does not depend on a small number of experts rescuing the work.

Peer Norms

What behaviors are reinforced or corrected by the group itself?

1. Peers address problems early instead of correcting them privately later.
2. Standards are reinforced consistently across the group.
3. Leaders are not the only people protecting quality.

Shared Capacity

Is there enough time, energy, and focus to do the work well?

1. Workloads are realistic given what is being asked.
2. Quality can hold during busy periods without constant heroics.
3. Leaders remove or defer work when demands exceed capacity.

System Cues

What does the organization actually reward, punish, or prioritize?

1. Metrics reflect what leadership says matters most.
2. Incentives and recognition support the desired outcome.
3. People are not rewarded for behavior leadership later complains about.

Tool Support

Do tools make the work easier or harder?

1. Tools reflect how the work is actually performed.
2. Tools reduce friction rather than creating extra effort.
3. Data from the system is trusted enough to guide decisions.

How to Read Your Results

Once you have rated the statements, review the pattern by lever.

Do not focus on the total score alone. Focus on where support is weakest.

Ask:

- Which lever received the lowest ratings most often?
- Which lever appears next weakest?
- Where did the scores vary the most?
- Which weak condition most directly affects the performance problem in front of us?

Your lowest lever is your likely primary constraint. Your next lowest lever may be reinforcing it.

If two levers seem tightly linked, begin with the one that shapes conditions rather than behavior. Fixing the environment usually makes behavior easier to change.

This matters because a weak score does not always mean the same kind of problem. Two teams can both score low on Shared Capacity for different reasons. One may be carrying too much work. Another may be carrying unclear work that keeps expanding. Two teams can both score low on Tool Support, but one may have a poor system design while another has a workable system layered with too many duplicate steps.

The diagnostic tells you where to look first. It does not eliminate the need for judgment.

A few common misreads are worth naming here.

- High effort does not equal high alignment.
- Low morale may reflect capacity or system cues rather than mindset.
- Tool frustration may point to design problems rather than unwillingness.
- More reminders do not create clarity if priorities were never ranked.
- More training does not build skill if overload prevents learning from sticking.

The goal is not to diagnose everything at once.

The goal is to find the condition that is most directly constraining results right now.

Once you have identified that condition, move to the chapter for that lever. Read it with your specific result in mind. If another lever appears to be reinforcing the problem, do not ignore that. Read both. Then use Chapter 20 to think carefully about sequence before you intervene.

This diagnostic is not designed to tell you what kind of leader you are.

It is designed to tell you where the work is breaking.

That distinction matters more than most organizations realize.

Chapter 14: Mindset Alignment

When priorities compete, do people know what matters most?

At Riverbend Health, the Patient Access Center looked like a performance problem. Wait times were rising. Patient complaints were increasing. Clinic leaders were frustrated by incomplete registrations and authorization issues that created downstream rework. Access Center leaders blamed workload. Clinic administrators blamed carelessness.

Andrea, the vice president of operations, brought the group together and asked a simple question.

"What is the primary objective of Patient Access right now?"

The answers came quickly, but they did not match.

- Reduce wait times.
- Schedule patients quickly so clinics stay full.
- Ensure registrations are accurate so clinics do not have to fix mistakes later.

Andrea asked the next question.

"Which one wins when they conflict?"

No one answered.

Over the next two weeks, she watched the system closely. Every morning, the Access Center huddled around a dashboard that treated speed as success. Leaders praised total calls handled and average handle time. Errors and rework were discussed later, usually after clinics complained.

Clinics, meanwhile, were measured on throughput and utilization. Missed appointments hurt clinic metrics immediately. Registration errors hurt later, in different places, and often landed on different people. No one owned the flow end to end.

The staff were not disengaged. They were trying to succeed. They moved calls quickly because that was the clearest visible signal in the system. When clinic staff pushed back, Access Center leaders reminded their team to be careful, but the system never resolved the tradeoff between speed and accuracy.

Andrea noticed something else. When priorities changed, leaders did not explain why. One week, leadership emphasized reducing wait times because of patient complaints. The next week, leadership emphasized authorization accuracy because of audit risk. Both priorities were valid. Neither was ranked. Staff were left to guess which mattered more in practice.

Andrea reviewed ten recent cases that had triggered complaints. In every case, the staff member had made a reasonable decision based on one definition of success. No one had ignored instructions. No one had violated policy.

The problem was not negligence.

The problem was that success had multiple, unspoken definitions.

Andrea wrote two statements on the whiteboard:

- Our primary objective is accurate scheduling and registration that prevents downstream rework.
- We will accept longer wait times temporarily while we stabilize accuracy.

Then she asked a different question.

"If this is true, what work stops, what work changes, and what do leaders stop praising?"

The discussion changed immediately. The dashboard needed to change. Rework had to become visible alongside speed. Clinics needed clearer intake standards. Leaders had to stop praising call volume without context. Staff needed a script for how to handle calls when authorizations could not be completed in real time.

The staff had not become more careful. The system had finally made its priorities explicit.

Within weeks, rework declined. Clinics reported fewer disruptions. Fewer errors created fewer follow-up calls. Wait times stabilized, not because staff worked harder, but because the system was creating less avoidable work.

This is Mindset Alignment.

Mindset Alignment exists when people understand what matters most, why it matters, and what should win when priorities collide. When it is strong, people can make sound decisions without constant oversight. When it is weak, leaders compensate with more reminders, more meetings, and more messaging. Those efforts rarely solve the problem because the issue is not message volume. The issue is unresolved tradeoffs.

When Mindset Alignment is weak, you may see:

- multiple reasonable answers to the same question about priorities
- different leaders making different decisions in similar situations
- direction changes without clear explanation
- teams that work hard but pull in different directions

How to Spot This Problem Early

This problem usually appears before results collapse.

Watch for small signs such as:

- leaders using different language to describe the same goal
- teams asking for repeated clarification on tradeoffs
- people escalating routine decisions because they do not know what should win
- frustration that sounds like "we keep changing direction" or "it depends who you ask"
- metrics that create different definitions of success in adjacent teams

These signs matter because Mindset Alignment problems often stay hidden while effort is still high. People can compensate for a while. They work harder, communicate more, and try to reconcile contradictions informally. Over time, though, those contradictions create inconsistent decisions, prevent learning, and increase friction between teams.

What Leaders Usually Get Wrong

Leaders often misread this as a communication problem.

They assume the issue is that people did not hear the message, so they repeat the message more often. They launch another meeting cadence. They restate the strategy. They send a clearer memo.

That can help if the issue was truly message transmission.

It does not help when the issue is that priorities were never actually resolved.

Mindset Alignment is not about whether leaders said something. It is about whether the system tells people what matters most when real tradeoffs appear. A team can hear the message perfectly and still make inconsistent decisions if leaders themselves have not ranked the priorities behind it.

Leaders also misread this as resistance when people ask repeated clarifying questions. In reality, those questions are often evidence that people are trying to act responsibly in a system that has not given them a stable decision rule.

Where to Start

Start by asking one question: What matters most in this work right now?

Write the answer in one sentence. Then test it. Ask three people in leadership and three people doing the work to answer the same question. If their answers differ, you have found the problem.

Then do three things:

- rank the top three priorities in order
- name what should happen when those priorities conflict
- remove or revise one measure, message, or expectation that points people in a different direction

If the priority is real, it should change what gets reinforced.

What Not to Do

Do not respond with more messaging alone.

More reminders will not fix a priority conflict that leadership has not resolved. Repeating the message more often can actually make things worse if the system still rewards something else. Before you communicate more clearly, make sure leadership itself is clear about what should win when tradeoffs appear.

Chapter 15: Skill Readiness

Do people have the knowledge and skill required to perform the work as designed?

Pinnacle Components won a contract to manufacture precision parts for an aerospace customer. The tolerances were tighter than anything the plant had produced before. The timeline was aggressive. Leadership was confident.

The operations director, Ben, believed the plant was ready. The operators were experienced. The supervisors were strong. The equipment was new. The assumption was simple: skilled people would adapt.

Within two weeks of launch, quality problems appeared at final inspection. The failures were not random. They clustered around a specific machining step that required a new measurement technique and a different calibration sequence. Rework increased. Scrap rates rose.

Ben responded quickly. He increased inspection frequency. He asked supervisors to double-check work. He emphasized the importance of quality in daily standups. Production slowed, but defects continued.

Supervisors began escalating work to Carla, a veteran technician. When Carla handled a batch, it passed. When she was unavailable, failures returned. Carla became a bottleneck. Schedules slipped.

Ben interpreted the pattern as an accountability issue.

"If Carla can do it, everyone should be able to do it."

Pressure increased. Operators became more cautious. Some slowed down. Others rushed and hoped inspection would catch problems. Quality did not stabilize.

Then Carla pulled Ben aside.

"This is not a discipline problem. The measurement process is new. The training they received was not enough."

Ben reviewed the training materials. What he found was thin. Training had consisted of a one-hour vendor presentation on launch day. The session explained the theory of the new method, but operators never practiced it with real parts. There was no competency check. There was no job aid at the machine. The calibration procedure sat in a shared folder that most operators could not access from the shop floor.

Supervisors had assumed experienced machinists would figure it out. Operators had assumed supervisors would correct them if they were wrong. Inspection caught failures, but too late to prevent rework.

Ben interviewed several operators privately. Their answers were consistent.

"I am not sure how much pressure to apply during measurement."
"I do not know when recalibration is required because guidance is

inconsistent."
"I do not want to stop the line to ask questions."

They were not describing unwillingness. They were describing uncertainty.

Ben tested his assumption. He selected six operators, gave them the same part, and asked each to perform the measurement. The variability was significant. The same part produced different results depending on who performed the task.

That was the real answer.

- This was not a motivation problem.
- This was not a compliance problem.
- This was a Skill Readiness problem.

Ben changed course. He paused production for two hours per shift for one week. During that time, Carla and a quality engineer demonstrated the measurement technique using actual production parts. Each operator practiced while being observed. Errors were corrected immediately. The team created a one-page job aid and posted it at each station.

Ben also changed expectations. Operators were not allowed to perform the step independently until they demonstrated consistency twice. Supervisors were instructed to treat questions as signals of responsibility, not weakness.

Within days, variability decreased. Defects dropped. Throughput recovered. Carla stopped being a bottleneck.

The improvement did not come from different people. It came from clearer conditions.

The system finally matched expectations with capability.

This is Skill Readiness.

Skill Readiness exists when people have the specific capability required for the work they are being asked to do now. When it is strong, quality improves with practice and support. When it is weak, pressure replaces learning and experts become bottlenecks.

When Skill Readiness is weak, you may see:

- recurring errors around specific tasks
- strong performance only when experts step in
- variability between people doing the same work
- training that is generic, late, or disconnected from real conditions

How to Spot This Problem Early

Skill Readiness problems rarely appear first as total failure. More often, they show up as inconsistency.

Watch for:

- one person consistently rescuing a task others struggle to perform
- errors clustering around one step instead of being spread across the whole process
- new expectations introduced without clear practice opportunities
- supervisors correcting mistakes repeatedly without seeing sustained improvement

Another early sign is overreliance on explanation. Leaders often assume that if something was explained, it was learned. That assumption becomes dangerous when the task requires judgment, repetition, calibration, or real-time adjustment.

What Leaders Usually Get Wrong

Leaders often misread this as low effort, weak accountability, or resistance.

They tell people to slow down and be more careful. They increase oversight. They remind everyone that quality matters. They hold people accountable for results the system never made them ready to produce.

Those actions can raise pressure, but they do not build skill.

Another common error is treating exposure as training. A walkthrough is not practice. A slide deck is not skill transfer. A launch-day explanation is not capability. If the work changed materially, then the learning process must change materially too.

Where to Start

Start with one recurring error, not the whole performance problem.

Identify the exact task where the error shows up. Then ask:

- what specific skill does this task require
- who can do it consistently
- how did they learn it
- where, exactly, are others getting stuck

Then check whether people have actually had the chance to learn this skill in a way that matches the real work. That means more than hearing an explanation. It means demonstration, practice, feedback, and a clear standard for acceptable performance.

A useful first move is to observe two people doing the same task and compare what they do differently. That usually tells you more than another discussion about accountability.

What Not to Do

Do not jump straight to pressure, reminders, or generic retraining.

If the issue is Skill Readiness, telling people to "be more careful" will not solve it. Neither will sending everyone through broad training that does not address the actual task breakdown. Focus on the specific capability the work requires, not on general effort or attitude.

Chapter 16: Peer Norms

What behaviors are reinforced or corrected by the group itself?

Summit Advisory was known for thoughtful client work and a collegial culture. Turnover was low. People described the firm as nice. Leaders took pride in the fact that teams got along.

Over time, client feedback began to shift. Deadlines slipped more often. Deliverables arrived with small but noticeable errors. Clients said things like, "We had to clarify this ourselves," and, "It took a few rounds to get it right."

Nothing looked dramatically broken in isolation.

Maya, a newly appointed practice leader, was asked to look into it. She reviewed staffing and timelines. The teams with the most issues were not understaffed or inexperienced. They used the same tools and templates as higher-performing teams.

Then Maya sat in on project meetings.

She noticed a pattern immediately. When a junior analyst presented a draft with gaps, peers nodded and moved on. When someone missed an internal deadline, another team member quietly fixed the work to keep the project on track. Feedback in meetings was vague.

> "This looks good."
> "We can tighten this later."

After meetings, the real work shifted into private correction. Senior analysts rewrote sections late at night. Managers cleaned up problems before clients saw them. The client received a polished deliverable, but extra hours piled up and frustration built.

Maya asked why issues were not raised earlier.

“We do not want to make things awkward,” one analyst said. “And some people have been here a long time. Calling them out does not go well.”

A manager added, “We have standards, but it is leadership’s job to enforce them. We do not want peers policing each other.”

That was the real pattern.

The firm’s peer norms rewarded keeping things smooth and quietly fixing problems. They did not reward early correction. When incomplete work was handed off, peers fixed it instead of sending it back. Over time, people learned that someone else would protect the standard for them.

Maya intervened with one project team. She set a simple rule: if a draft had gaps, send it back with the standard that was missed. She also changed recognition. Teams that delivered clean work on the first pass were praised. Peers who named issues early were recognized.

At first, the team was uncomfortable. Then quality improved. Deadlines stabilized. Late-night rework declined.

The culture did not become harsh.

It became clearer.

Peers began to protect standards because standards now protected them.

This is Peer Norms.

Peer Norms shape what the group itself reinforces, tolerates, or corrects without waiting for management. When this lever is strong, quality is protected early. When it is weak, leaders become the only enforcement mechanism and peers learn to rescue rather than correct.

When Peer Norms are weak, you may see:

- leaders as the first responders to quality problems
- peers quietly fixing one another's work
- vague feedback in meetings and blunt feedback in private
- uneven standards based on tenure, popularity, or status

How to Spot This Problem Early

Peer Norm problems usually show up first in the gap between what is said in the room and what happens after the meeting.

Watch for:

- meetings where concerns are implied but rarely stated directly
- strong performers carrying quiet cleanup work for the group
- recurring issues that "somehow" keep getting fixed without formal correction

- standards that depend on who produced the work, not on the work itself
- leaders learning about quality problems later than peers do

One of the clearest early signals is private frustration paired with public politeness. When people complain in side conversations but avoid naming the issue where the work is being shaped, peer norms are likely protecting comfort more than performance.

What Leaders Usually Get Wrong

Leaders often misread this as culture in the vaguest sense.

They say the team needs more trust, more openness, or more candor. They hold a discussion about values. They ask people to speak up more.

Those moves are not harmful on their own, but they are usually too abstract.

Peer Norms are not changed by aspiration alone. They change when the group learns what it is expected to reinforce, what it is expected to correct, and what will happen when someone does name a problem early.

Another common mistake is assuming that niceness is the same as health. A polite team can still have weak peer norms if quality is being protected privately rather than collectively.

Where to Start

Start with an issue the team already sees but doesn't address directly.

Look for the work that gets quietly corrected, the deadline that keeps slipping without open discussion, or the weak handoff that others keep compensating for. Name the standard being missed as clearly as you can.

Then decide what peers should do the next time it happens. Keep it simple and specific. For example:

- return incomplete work instead of fixing it silently
- name the missed standard in the meeting where the work is reviewed
- ask one direct question before the problem moves downstream

The goal is not confrontation for its own sake. The goal is to stop teaching the team that someone else will quietly absorb the cost.

What Not to Do

Do not assume this will improve through culture talk alone.

A general conversation about trust, openness, or candor will not change peer behavior unless people also know what they are expected to reinforce and correct in real time. Keep the conversation tied to specific work standards, not abstract values.

Chapter 17: Shared Capacity

Is there enough time, energy, and focus to do the work well?

The County Benefits Office was behind. Eligibility determinations were taking weeks longer than required by policy. Complaints had reached elected officials. Leadership pressure increased with every news story.

From the outside, it looked like a productivity problem.

Inside the office, it felt different.

Caseworkers arrived early and left late. Overtime was routine. Lunch breaks were skipped. Supervisors thanked people for pushing through. Still, the backlog grew.

Jordan, the deputy director, was asked to get things under control. He started by listening.

Supervisors said they needed people to work faster. Caseworkers said they could not keep up.

"Every time we get ahead, something new hits."

Jordan looked at the work itself. Each caseworker was managing new applications, recertifications, appeals, and corrections, all with different deadlines and complexity. New work entered continuously. Nothing ever stopped.

He asked a simple question in a staff meeting.

"How many active cases are you working right now?"

The answers varied widely. Some said twenty. Others said forty. A few said they had stopped counting.

Capacity was not defined or tracked consistently.

Jordan reviewed three months of data. Error rates spiked during high-volume periods. Those errors created rework, which increased workload further. Pressure made the system less effective, not more.

Leadership's response had been additive. They added tracking reports, check-ins, and daily targets. None of those actions removed work.

Caseworkers adapted by juggling dozens of cases at once. They touched everything partially. Focus dropped. Small mistakes increased, not because people were careless, but because they were exhausted and fragmented.

Urgency became permanent. Everything felt critical. Nothing was meaningfully prioritized.

Jordan reframed the problem.

"This is not a motivation issue. This is not a skill issue. This is a capacity issue."

He proposed a controlled change. For one month, the office would limit work in progress. Each caseworker would carry a defined number of active cases. New intake would continue, but cases would be staged instead of assigned immediately. The goal was to finish work cleanly instead of touching everything at once.

Jordan also removed work. Two internal reports that did not drive decisions were paused. One recurring meeting was eliminated. Supervisors were instructed to surface capacity limits instead of hiding them.

The first week was uncomfortable. Output dipped slightly. Leadership worried.

Jordan held steady.

Error rates declined. Rework dropped. By the third week, completed cases increased. The backlog began to move because the system had stopped creating new work through mistakes.

Caseworkers still worked hard.

They were no longer drowning.

Their resilience was never the constraint. The load was.

Capacity limits were finally acknowledged.

This is Shared Capacity.

Shared Capacity exists when the system provides enough time, energy, and focus for people to do the work well. When it is strong, quality can hold under pressure. When it is weak, speed replaces judgment and burnout becomes normal.

When Shared Capacity is weak, you may see:

- too many active items in progress at once
- errors increasing during peak periods

- rework rising with volume
- overtime and exhaustion treated as normal
- leaders adding controls without removing work

How to Spot This Problem Early

Shared Capacity problems usually appear before people say they are overwhelmed.

Watch for:

- unfinished work accumulating across multiple priorities
- more items started than completed
- strong people becoming slower, less precise, or more reactive under load
- recurring delays during predictable busy periods
- basic work quality dropping when new tasks are added, even when no one is openly resisting

Another early sign is invisible triage. People begin making private decisions about what can slip, what can be deferred, and what can be approximated because the official workload no longer fits the available time and attention. When that happens, the system has already exceeded usable capacity, even if no one has said so directly.

You may also hear language that sounds responsible on the surface but signals strain underneath:

- "We are doing our best."
- "It is just a busy season."

- "We will catch up next week."
- "We only need everyone to push a little harder."

When those statements repeat over time, they often describe a structural condition, not a temporary surge.

What Leaders Usually Get Wrong

Leaders often misread this as a commitment problem.

They assume the team needs to be more disciplined, more efficient, or more resilient. They ask people to prioritize better without reducing the number of priorities. They add tracking and oversight to gain control, not realizing those actions consume even more time and attention.

Another common error is mistaking visible busyness for usable capacity. A team can look active, responsive, and dedicated while still operating far beyond the point where quality can hold. In fact, heroic effort often hides Shared Capacity problems longer than it solves them.

Leaders also underestimate the cost of fragmentation. When people are switching constantly between tasks, deadlines, and interruptions, the issue is not just the amount of work. The issue is that attention is being broken into pieces too small to support good judgment.

Where to Start

Start by making the load visible.

Ask each person to list the active work they are currently carrying, not just their official responsibilities. Then compare the lists. Look for too much work in progress, hidden rework, and tasks that were added without anything being removed.

Once that is visible, make one real reduction. For example:

- pause one low-value report
- cancel one recurring meeting that does not change decisions
- delay one noncritical initiative
- cap the number of active items one team can carry at a time

If nothing changes about the amount of work, Shared Capacity will not improve just because people understand the problem better.

What Not to Do

Do not respond with resilience advice, time management tips, or encouragement to push harder.

Those responses treat overload as a personal weakness to manage instead of a system condition to correct. If the system is carrying more work than people can do well, the answer is not better coping. The answer is reducing, sequencing, or redesigning the load.

Chapter 18: System Cues

What does the organization actually reward, punish, or prioritize?

Brightline Software was growing quickly. New customer bookings were strong. Leadership was proud of the sales team's energy and ambition.

At the same time, customer churn was creeping up.

Customer success leaders reported a familiar pattern. New clients arrived with expectations that did not match reality. Features were implied that were not part of the product. Timelines were promised without delivery input. Implementations started behind schedule, and relationships were strained before value was delivered.

The CEO addressed the issue directly in an all-hands meeting.

"We need to stop overselling. Long-term trust matters more than short-term wins."

Heads nodded. The message was clear.

Two weeks later, nothing changed.

Sales reps continued to push aggressive deals. Customer success continued to clean up the mess. Product teams continued to get blamed for scope gaps they had not created.

From leadership's perspective, the behavior was baffling.

Given the incentives in place, it was completely predictable.

Alex, the chief revenue officer, decided to look past intent and examine the mechanics.

He started with compensation. Sales commissions were heavily weighted toward new bookings. Renewals mattered, but they represented a much smaller portion of total pay. Deals closed faster when scope was loose. There was no direct consequence for downstream pain, because that pain showed up after commission had already been paid.

Alex looked at reporting cadence. Every Monday, leadership reviewed a dashboard. The first metric discussed was bookings. Renewal health was reviewed monthly and framed as a customer success issue. Sales leaders did not experience renewal outcomes as part of their operating reality.

Alex interviewed several sales reps privately.

"I know retention matters, but my job is to close."
"If I slow down to get everything perfect, I miss my number."
"Customer success will fix it later."

These were not bad actors.

They were rational actors responding to cues.

Then Alex examined recognition. At quarterly meetings, top sellers were celebrated publicly. The stories highlighted deal size and speed. No one told stories about clean handoffs or long-term fit. New reps quickly learned what success looked like in practice.

Alex saw the full picture.

The organization said it valued long-term trust.

The system rewarded something else.

Alex proposed a change that made leadership uncomfortable. A meaningful portion of compensation would now be tied to renewal health at six and twelve months. Complex deals would require an implementation readiness check framed as shared ownership, not approval overhead. Recognition would shift toward deals with strong fit, accurate expectations, and clean handoffs.

There was resistance. A few top performers left. Leadership worried.

Six months later, churn stabilized. Customer success reported fewer escalations. Sales cycles lengthened slightly, but deal quality improved. The organization stopped acting surprised by behavior it had previously rewarded.

The stated values had not changed. The cues finally matched them.

This is System Cues.

System Cues shape behavior through metrics, incentives, processes, recognition, and leadership attention. When this lever is strong, behavior aligns naturally with stated goals. When it is weak, leaders speak one set of values while the system teaches another.

When System Cues are weak, you may see:

- behavior that repeatedly contradicts stated priorities
- metrics that pull people in competing directions

- gaming that surprises leaders but makes sense to everyone else
- recognition patterns that reward the wrong wins

How to Spot This Problem Early

System Cue problems usually show up before leaders are ready to admit the system is teaching the wrong lesson.

Watch for:

- repeated behavior that leadership says it does not want, but continues to reward indirectly
- people describing success in the language of numbers, incentives, or visibility rather than mission or customer value
- one set of priorities in official messaging and a different set in meetings, dashboards, and recognition
- predictable workarounds or gaming that leaders describe as disappointing but employees describe as practical
- frustration from one part of the system cleaning up consequences created by another part

Another early sign is leadership surprise. When leaders keep saying, “I do not understand why people are doing this,” the better question is often, “What makes this behavior rational in the current system?”

That is the key distinction. System Cue problems are rarely mysterious from the inside. They only look irrational from a distance.

What Leaders Usually Get Wrong

Leaders often misread this as a values problem.

They respond with speeches, statements, and stronger language about what the organization believes. They remind people what good behavior looks like. They restate expectations and assume the issue is moral commitment.

That rarely works if the system keeps rewarding the opposite.

Another common mistake is focusing only on formal incentives. Compensation matters, but it is not the whole picture. System Cues also include what gets measured first, what gets questioned in meetings, what gets celebrated publicly, what leaders notice, and what leaders let slide when results are strong.

People learn quickly from what the system pays attention to, not just from what the handbook says.

Where to Start

Start with one behavior leadership says it wants to stop.

Then trace what makes that behavior sensible in the current system. Look at:

- what gets measured first
- what gets rewarded
- what gets praised publicly
- what people get pressured on in the moment
- what leaders tolerate when results look good

Pick one cue and change it. That might mean revising a metric, changing how success is recognized, or shifting what leadership reviews first in meetings. You do not need to redesign the entire system at once, but you do need to change something people can actually feel.

If the cue structure stays the same, the behavior usually will too.

What Not to Do

Do not rely on stronger messaging about values or expectations alone.

People pay close attention to what the system rewards, not just what leadership says it wants. If incentives, dashboards, and recognition still point in the wrong direction, better language will not solve the problem. Change the cue, then reinforce the message.

Chapter 19: Tool Support

Do tools make the work easier or harder?

Stonebridge Construction rolled out a new project management platform across all active job sites. Leadership expected the system to improve schedule accuracy, cost control, and visibility. The rollout was fast. Configuration decisions were made centrally. Field supervisors were told the tool would standardize how work was done.

Within the first month, leadership was frustrated.

Dashboards were incomplete. Updates were missing. Schedules did not reflect reality. Executives concluded that field teams were not adopting the tool. Training reminders were sent. Usage expectations were reiterated.

Nothing improved.

Tara, the director of project controls, decided to spend time in the field. She rode along with two site supervisors for a full day and watched how work actually happened.

The supervisors started the day with the platform open, but they did not rely on it. They relied on notebooks, phone calls, and a shared spreadsheet maintained by a foreman.

When Tara asked why, one supervisor answered plainly.

"The system does not match how we run work."

She watched a supervisor try to log a delay. The platform required several fields that did not fit the situation. Connectivity dropped. The entry froze. After the second failure, the supervisor stopped trying and wrote a note instead.

Later, Tara noticed something more serious. The platform schedule assumed ideal conditions. Materials arrived on time. Subcontractors were available as planned. Permits were issued as expected. None of those assumptions held consistently in the field.

The moment reality diverged from the plan, the system became inaccurate. Once the system was inaccurate, people stopped trusting it. Once they stopped trusting it, they stopped updating it. Leadership saw missing data and concluded the people were the problem.

Workarounds appeared quickly.

Foremen tracked subcontractor commitments in spreadsheets. Crews coordinated changes through text messages. Procurement maintained a separate log of deliveries because partial shipments were not represented well in the system. The same information was entered multiple times in multiple places.

These workarounds were not sabotage.

They were survival.

Tara interviewed supervisors privately.

"I would use the system if it saved me time."

"I cannot afford to fight the tool during the day."

"I update it later, but later never really comes."

Tara compared system data to actual job activity. The gap was wide. She calculated the time being spent reconciling conflicting information across systems. The cost was significant.

Leadership had been asking the wrong question.

They had been asking, "Why will people not use the tool?"

They should have been asking, "Why does the work require so many workarounds?"

Tara reframed the intervention. She mapped the real workflow from the field perspective. She removed nonessential fields and reduced steps required for updates. She aligned schedule logic with real constraints, including permits and subcontractor lead times. Then she set a clear rule: leadership would not punish missing data until the tool reflected reality.

Adoption increased almost immediately.

Supervisors trusted the system because it mirrored their work. Updates became part of the day instead of a separate task. Workarounds declined. Leadership visibility improved.

People did not become more compliant.

The tool was redesigned to match how the work was actually done.

This is Tool Support.

Tool Support exists when tools reflect real workflows, reduce friction, produce trusted information, and evolve as the work changes. When it is strong, people can complete work cleanly inside the system. When it is weak, they create shadow systems, duplicate entry, and manual checks just to get through the day.

When Tool Support is weak, you may see:

- spreadsheets or notes outside the main system
- repeated entry of the same information
- reports people do not trust
- workarounds that become normal
- training demands that never seem to solve the problem

How to Spot This Problem Early

Tool Support problems often appear first as annoyance, delay, or quiet workaround behavior.

Watch for:

- people keeping side files even when the official system is available
- manual checks before decisions are made because the data is not trusted

- duplicate entry across systems, spreadsheets, or handwritten notes
- updates being delayed until the end of the day, the end of the week, or "when there is time"
- complaints that sound like user resistance but consistently reference friction, steps, missing options, or inaccurate outputs

Another early sign is selective use. People use some parts of the system and avoid others. That usually means the tool fits one part of the workflow and distorts another. It is a clue worth studying, not a compliance issue to shut down.

You may also notice that high performers are the fastest to develop workarounds. That is not because they are unwilling. It is often because they feel the cost of friction first and solve for it immediately.

What Leaders Usually Get Wrong

Leaders often misread this as an adoption problem.

They assume the tool is fine and the people are failing to use it correctly. The response is predictable: more training, stronger mandates, tighter compliance checks, and repeated reminders about standardization.

That can raise usage statistics without improving work.

Another common mistake is treating system accuracy as a user responsibility when the system itself is structurally hard to keep accurate. If updating the tool takes too long, requires unrealistic assumptions, or fails to reflect how decisions are actually made, the people closest to the work will route around it.

Leaders also underestimate the trust problem. Once users learn that the system does not reflect reality, adoption becomes more than a training issue. It becomes a credibility issue.

Where to Start

Start by watching the work, not by reviewing the tool documentation.

Sit with one person using the system in real time. Ask them to complete a normal task and talk through where the tool helps, where it slows them down, and where they switch to another method. Pay attention to workarounds, repeated entry, delays, and places where people stop trusting the output.

Then make one practical improvement. For example:

- remove one unnecessary field
- eliminate one duplicate entry step
- simplify one update process
- fix one part of the workflow people avoid whenever they can

You are looking for friction that the system created, not just user habits you can correct.

What Not to Do

Do not assume the first answer is more training or tighter compliance.

If people are working around the tool, there is usually a reason. Mandates may increase visible usage while leaving the real problem untouched. Before asking for better adoption, make sure the tool actually supports the work people are being asked to do.

Chapter 20: Lever Interactions

Why fixing one thing rarely fixes the system.

By this point, you may feel ready to act.

You can see the evidence. You have identified a likely lever under strain. You know where the work appears to be breaking down.

This is where many leaders stumble.

They fix the right thing, but in the wrong order. Or they improve one condition while leaving another condition in place that quietly cancels the gain. The result is familiar: brief improvement, partial compliance, and then a slow return to old patterns.

The JL^3 Performance Levers™ are not a checklist. They are interacting forces. When one lever weakens, it often places strain on another. When leaders ignore that interaction, they mistake stalled improvement for resistance, inconsistency, or poor follow-through.

A team may genuinely need stronger skills. But if overload leaves no room to learn, the new learning will not stick. A leader may clarify priorities well, but if System Cues still reward a different outcome, the clarity will not survive contact with the work. A tool may be trainable in theory, but if the tool fights the workflow, people will comply only on the surface.

This is why strong interventions sometimes fail.

They solve part of the problem.

Then the rest of the system pulls the old behavior back into place.

Why Leaders Choose the Wrong Lever First

Leaders rarely begin with the wrong lever because they are careless. They begin there because the wrong lever often looks more visible, more manageable, or more familiar.

- Skill problems are easy to imagine because training is a known response.
- Communication problems are easy to name because messaging is fast.
- Accountability problems are attractive because they preserve a sense of managerial control.
- Tool problems are often misread as user problems because that keeps the system design out of question.

In other words, leaders often choose the lever that gives them the quickest feeling of action, not the lever that most accurately explains the result.

That is why this framework matters. It helps interrupt the reflex to act on the most emotionally satisfying explanation.

When the diagnostic points to two weak levers, the lower score tells you where strain is most visible. It does not automatically tell you where to begin.

Start by asking a second question: Which weak condition is making the other one harder to fix?

A team may score low on Skill Readiness because people are making preventable errors. That matters. But if the same team also scores low on Shared Capacity, overload may be the reason learning is not sticking. People may not have enough time, attention, or recovery to practice, absorb feedback, and improve. In that case, the skill problem is real, but capacity is the better place to begin.

The same pattern shows up elsewhere. A team may score low on Mindset Alignment because priorities feel unclear. That confusion may be real. But if System Cues are also weak, people may be responding rationally to incentives, metrics, or recognition that point in another direction. In that case, clearer messaging is unlikely to hold until the cues change.

The scores help you locate weaknesses. They do not replace judgment about sequence. In this framework, judgment means asking which weak condition is making improvement harder in the other area.

When two levers score low, begin with the one that is shaping the conditions around the other. Fix the environment that is reinforcing the problem first. Then address the behavior or capability that has been weakened inside it.

That is how leaders avoid solving one real problem while leaving the surrounding system strong enough to pull the old pattern back into place.

Common Interaction Patterns

Shared Capacity before Skill Readiness

Training added on top of chronic overload does not create capability. It creates one more burden to absorb.

When expectations increase before skills catch up, errors rise. Leaders respond with urgency. Capacity erodes further. Experts rescue work. Improvement appears briefly, then collapses.

Interrupt this loop by reducing load enough for learning to happen. Build capability in conditions where people can actually practice, retain, and apply what they are being asked to learn.

Never build skills on top of chronic overload.

Tool Support before Skill Readiness

New tools that do not fit the actual workflow create frustration instead of consistent use.

Leaders often respond to stalled performance by mandating tool use. People comply visibly while creating shadow systems underneath. Usage metrics improve. Outcomes do not.

Interrupt this loop by first asking whether the tool reflects real work. If it does not, redesign comes before deeper training. Training people to use a poor fit more faithfully does not solve the problem.

Do not enforce tools people cannot use well in context.

System Cues before Mindset Alignment

Leaders clarify priorities, but incentives still reward something else.

People follow the incentives. Leaders accuse them of not listening. Cynicism grows. The message may be clear, but the rewards contradict it.

Interrupt this loop by auditing incentives, metrics, and recognition before launching a clarity campaign. If the system pays for one result and talks about another, people will learn which one is real.

Never ask people to ignore the scoreboard.

System Cues before Peer Norms

Leaders want peers to reinforce better standards, but the system still rewards the wrong outcomes.

In those conditions, peers end up absorbing the cost of quality while others keep benefiting from speed, volume, or visibility. Quiet resentment grows. Standards become uneven.

When peer norms or system cues are weak, high performers often become the unofficial safety net. They correct avoidable mistakes, carry extra follow-up, answer repeated questions, and absorb the strain required to keep quality from dropping. Leaders may see steady results without realizing those results are being held together by a small number of people carrying work that should have been shared.

Interrupt this loop by fixing the cue structure first. Peer correction is more sustainable when the system does not punish the people trying to uphold the standard.

Social pressure cannot reliably overcome structural contradictions.

Shared Capacity and Mindset Alignment

Everything is labeled a priority. Nothing is removed. Focus fragments. Quality declines. Leaders respond by clarifying expectations while continuing to overload the system.

This creates a painful cycle. People hear the priorities clearly, but they still cannot execute them consistently because the work volume makes tradeoffs impossible in practice.

Interrupt this loop by ranking priorities and removing work at the same time. Clarity without relief can increase frustration because it makes the contradiction easier to see.

If everything matters, nothing is clear.

How to Spot Interaction Problems Early

Interaction problems often appear when a reasonable intervention produces only partial results.

Watch for:

- early improvement followed by drift
- one team improving while another still struggles under the same initiative
- strong agreement with a change effort but weak follow-through in practice
- leaders concluding that "the problem must be attitude" because the first intervention did not stick

- repeated cycles of trying a new fix every few months without stable improvement

These signs matter because they suggest the first diagnosis may have been incomplete rather than totally wrong.

In many cases, the leader did identify a real issue. They just did not identify the reinforcing condition working against it.

How to Sequence Action

When diagnosing a performance problem:

- identify the lever where strain is most visible
- identify the second weak lever that may be reinforcing it
- ask which weak conditions are making improvement more difficult in the other area
- begin with that lever

In general:

- fix Shared Capacity before Skill Readiness
- fix Tool Support before Skill Readiness
- fix System Cues before Mindset Alignment
- fix System Cues before Peer Norms

This order matters because condition-setting levers determine whether behavior change can hold.

Leaders do not need perfect certainty before acting. But they do need enough clarity to avoid solving one piece of the problem while leaving the surrounding conditions intact.

Final Rule

If an intervention produces a brief improvement and then the old pattern returns, do not assume the people involved failed to follow through. More often, the first change addressed one real problem while leaving another condition in place that continued to reinforce the old behavior. When that happens, the task is not to blame the people or repeat the same intervention with more force. The task is to ask what in the surrounding system is still making the old pattern easier to sustain than the new one. That is the loop leaders need to find.

From Insight to Action

By now, you have seen the six levers individually and in combination. You have also seen a central truth running through this book: performance problems rarely come from people alone. More often, they come from the conditions surrounding the work.

That does not mean every problem requires a complete redesign. It means the next step is to look carefully and respond with intention.

Start by identifying where friction is highest. Look for the condition that is making consistent performance harder than it should be. In some cases, that will be a clear skill gap. In others, it will be an unclear expectation, a broken handoff, an outdated cue, or a tool that creates more work than it removes. Sometimes one lever stands out immediately. Sometimes several are interacting at once.

Do not make the mistake of trying to fix everything at the same time.

The goal is not to overhaul the entire system overnight. The goal is to make the next useful decision. Address the lever that is creating the most strain. Watch what changes. Then look again.

Better performance does not usually come from one dramatic intervention. It comes from a series of more accurate choices about how the work is designed, supported, and reinforced.

Companion Resources

If you would like additional tools to help you apply the ideas in this book, companion resources are available online.

These materials are designed to help you work through the framework more practically, reflect on the six levers, and begin diagnosing where performance may be breaking down in your own environment.

Available resources include:

- The JL^3 Performance Levers™ Quick Reference
- Performance Stall Quick Diagnostic
- Where to Start When Performance Stalls

To access the companion resources, visit:

www.jl3learningsolutions.com/whenperformancestalls

Use these tools as a starting point. The goal is not to complete more worksheets. The goal is to see the work more clearly, identify the conditions shaping performance, and take a more informed first step.

Acknowledgments

This book exists because of the people who shaped me, supported me, and encouraged me along the way.

To my husband, thank you for your steady support through the long process of developing this methodology and writing this book. Your encouragement and belief in me gave me the space to keep going.

To my mom, thank you for laying the foundation for so much of who I am. You taught me that there is a right way to do things, and that belief has shaped how I work, how I lead, and how I approached building something meant to help others.

To my sons, thank you for your love and patience as this book took shape. Your support meant more than you know.

To Michelle, Sara, Josh, and Melissa, thank you for your encouragement, feedback, and honesty throughout this process. This book is stronger because you were willing to listen, challenge my thinking, and help me refine what I was trying to build. Your belief in this work helped me carry it forward.

I am also grateful for the professional, leadership, and service experiences that shaped my thinking over the years. Each one contributed in different ways through formal development, practical lessons, and the daily work of leading, learning, and solving real problems. Those experiences stretched my thinking, deepened my leadership, and helped shape this work.

And to my readers, thank you for picking up this book. I hope what is here helps you see your work more clearly, apply these ideas in a practical way, and create better results for the people and teams you lead.

If you enjoyed this book, please consider leaving a review on our Amazon site.

About the Author

Jennifer Lilly is the founder of JL^{3} Learning Solutions and the creator of the JL^{3} Performance Levers™, a framework for understanding how the conditions of work shape team performance.

Her perspective is grounded in a longstanding interest in how people, processes, and systems interact to produce results. Jennifer studied social science and public administration as an undergraduate and later earned a Master of Public Administration with an executive leadership focus. She also studied instructional design through the Association for Talent Development, holds a Six Sigma Green Belt certification, and earned a Systems Thinking Certificate from Cornell University. Together, those experiences shaped the practical and structural lens behind her work.

Across her career, Jennifer has worked in and alongside complex organizations where performance problems were often attributed to motivation, engagement, or accountability. Repeatedly, she observed that capable, committed people struggled not because they lacked effort, but because the systems around them made success difficult to sustain. That insight led to the development of the JL^{3} Performance Levers™, a six-lever framework that examines how mindset alignment, skill readiness, peer norms, shared capacity, system cues, and tool support interact to shape performance.

When Performance Stalls is her first book.

Jennifer lives in Iowa.

www.ingramcontent.com/pod-product-compliance
Ingram Content Group UK Ltd.
Pitfield, Milton Keynes, MK11 3LW, UK
UKHW022026190726
13853UKWH00005B/2131

THINKING IN CHINESE MEDICINE

A Patient's Guide to Acupuncture

DR JORDAN BARBER, DAOM

DR PETER CARON, DACM

ISBN (hardcover): 979-8-9919113-7-5

ISBN (ebook): 979-8-9919113-8-2

ISBN (paperback): 979-8-9919113-9-9

Library of Congress Control Number: 2026906513

Published by Dymphna Publishing

First edition

Contents